Dedication

This book is dedicated to Robert Rodale, a member of the board of advisors of the Made in the USA Foundation, who was a champion of personal and national self-reliance.

Acknowledgments

Hundreds of people were involved in the preparation of this book, and we regret that we can not mention them all by name. Every company mentioned in this book provided necessary information. We thank all of the manufacturers for providing us with the photographs that were selected; all photographs were provided to us as a courtesy of the manufacturer of the product shown.

The staff of the Made in the USA Foundation, especially executive director Chris Burke and chairman Joel D. Joseph; Ayfir Jafri, Jeff Blaydes, Eddie Meng and Alan Sultan, made thousands of phone calls checking out products and visiting hundreds of retail stores.

We would like to thank Debbie Wager, Ben Giliberti and Mike Ferrara for writing their excellent chapters. Michael Joseph added the information on American video games. We are indebted to Rich Ceppos, Executive Editor of *Car and Driver* for his recommendations.

Sarah Kim Chang, Lisa McClelland, Phil Martin of Murray Manufacturing Co., John Kukudo of *Bicycling* magazine, Jim Sweet of Emerson Marketing, the Motorcycle Industry Council, Tom Cook of *Cellular Business* magazine, Tom Armstrong of Cannondale Bicycle Co. and Jon Streeter of the U.S. Commerce Department were all helpful in providing us with facts, figures and other information.

MADE IN THE USA

The Complete Guide To America's Finest Products

1991 EDITION

by the
Made In the USA Foundation

National
Press
Books

Library of Congress Cataloging-in-Publication Data

Made in the USA:
The complete guide to America's finest products
by the Made in the USA Foundation.
295 p., 15 cm. x 23 cm.
Includes index.
ISBN 0-915765-71-3: $9.95
1. Consumer education--United States.
2. Commercial products--United States--Catalogs.
I. Made in the USA Foundation.
TX336.M33
381'.45'000973--dc20
89-12672
CIP

PRINTED IN THE UNITED STATES OF AMERICA
1991 Edition

3

Table of Contents

Made in the USA Foundation

The Made in the USA Foundation prepared this book to provide consumers with information about the best products that America has to offer. Use of this information is intended to reduce imports to the United States and to encourage exports of high-quality U.S. goods.

This book will be updated and revised every year. But this book is only the first step in a continuing effort to mobilize consumers, increase awareness and prompt action to improve America's standing in the world economy.

The Made in the USA Foundation is a membership organization of American consumers, trade unions, manufacturers and associations founded on the premise that action must be taken to reduce U.S. reliance on imports, to increase purchases of American products domestically and overseas and to ensure that the standard of fair trade is applied evenly around the globe.

The Foundation's objective is to change government policies, consumer behavior and corporate practices that have contributed to America's decline in the international marketplace, with the goal of a significant reduction of the U.S. trade deficit by the year 2000.

In addition to publishing this book and promoting consumer awareness, the Foundation is sponsoring other activities to improve American competitiveness. The Foundation circulates a quarterly newsletter to members informing them of issues and progress, as well as updated information on the best American products. The Foundation investigates and researches current trade and competitiveness issues and prepares reports with recommendation for government and private action. The Foundation also promotes American products by publicity in the media and with its "American Showcase" displays around the world. The Foundation's Corporate Matchmaker Program puts manufacturers and retailers together.

To join the Made in the USA Foundation contact us at:

Made in the USA Foundation
7200 Wisconsin Avenue
Bethesda, Maryland 20814
(301) 657-1618
(800) USA-PRIDE

☆　☆　☆　☆　☆

Chapter One

Introduction

☆　☆　☆　☆　☆

This is the second edition of *Made in the USA: A Catalog of the Best American Products*. We have added hundreds of new products to the book, made numerous corrections and other improvements, and will continue to do so every year.

Why Do Consumers Need This Book?

We (the Made in the USA Foundation) have heard comments from many consumers who say: "why shouldn't I just buy the best product available, no matter where it is made?" First of all it is not always easy to determine what the best product, or even the cheapest product, is. We believe that <u>most</u> of the time the best American product is the best product in the world of the same type. There are at least ten reasons why it is in your own best interest to buy American:

Ten Reasons to Buy American

1. American products are designed for American physiques and standards;
2. American products are safer;
3. U.S. products represent the best values;
4. Consumer protection laws are better here and U.S. companies are more concerned with consumer's rights;
5. U.S. warranties are better;
6. Workers who made American products are earning decent wages (no slave labor here);
7. Working conditions of workers are better in the U.S. than abroad;
8. U.S. products are made in compliance with environmental laws;
9. Replacement parts are available at reasonable prices;
10. If you don't buy American you will pay higher taxes for unemployment and welfare benefits.

Not all of these ten reasons apply to every product. American products, such as clothing, often fit better because they were designed for American physiques. If a replacement part is needed for an American appliance or automobile, it is usually more readily available, and at a better price, than an imported part. American warranties are usually better than foreign ones. Many American products have lifetime warranties (for example, Sears Craftsmen hand tools).

When you buy an American-made product you can be assured that the workers who made it were treated properly. In China, for example, many "workers" are actually political prisoners forced to work in a sweat shop. Our occupational safety and health laws are the toughest in the world.

Our consumer protection laws are the strictest in the world, as are our environmental standards. Pesticides that are banned in the United States are contained on imported tomatoes from Mexico. Japan, except for automobiles, has no laws governing recalls of defective consumer products. During the beginning of 1990 four Japanese electronic giants, Sony, Panasonic, Pioneer and Toshiba, issued nationwide recalls in the U.S. for hundreds of thousands of color televisions that posed a fire danger. According to Michiko Aoyama, of the Japan Consumer Information Center, "safety for consumers has been ignored" in Japan. As you will learn from our chapter on automobiles, American cars are the safest in the world.

All things considered, when you buy an American-made product you get the most value for your dollar. Most consumers do not realize that the United States has the highest productivity of any nation in the world and remains the largest exporting country. Our productivity and market size allow us to bring mass market valued to your home

You will notice that none of the ten reasons for buying American is for patriotism. We don't expect you to buy American products for patriotism alone, and that is the reason that we have sought only the best American products.

This book was written by the staff of the Made in the USA Foundation to inform consumers of the best American-made products available. The Foundation consulted experts in many fields before recommending specific products, and for three chapters independent experts were hired to review the best American products in their field. The authors of these three chapters (on trucks, toys and wine and beer) are noted in the chapter.

Many consumers overseas know that by buying American products they are buying high-quality products at a reasonable price. Whatever the reason for buying American, this book can help you make informed purchasing decisions. A recent survey in Poland showed that Poles preferred American products to Polish-made products.

Misconceptions, misconceptions

There is a widespread misconception that very few products are still made in the United States. In fact, many of the finest manufactured products are still made in the U.S. As this book demonstrates, many of the finest automobiles, computers, telephone equipment, bicycles, clothing, shoes, sporting goods, musical instruments and stereo equipment are American-made.

Contrary to popular misconception, U.S. high technology products are among the best in the world. Most people do not realize that the U.S. electronics industry is still the largest in the world, slightly ahead of Japan's. In many areas the United States leads the world in technology and quality. Japan's national telephone company, Nippon Telephone and Telegraph Company, is buying "state of the art" equipment from AT&T. Kimio Tazaki, executive director of NT&T's Network Systems Development Center, says "AT&T has the most advanced technology in the world."

We still make quality products in the United States, but many consumers have no idea which products are made here. We have only one major television manufacturer left in the United States—do you know who it is? Some of the best automobiles, and the best automotive values, are made right here. Some of the finest, and reasonably-priced clothing and shoes are made right here. Some of the best computers, stereo and other high tech equipment are made in the United States, and sold around the world.

U.S.A.-made beer and wine are world-class. Wines from California and other states equal or surpass the great wines of Europe.

The United States leads the world in developing sporting goods and exercise equipment, stereo speakers, blue jeans, food—an endless variety of products. You could live very comfortably with only goods made in the United States.

Finding Out What is Made in the USA

One problem in purchasing American products is discovering the country of origin of the item. Many American corporations, including AT&T, IBM, General Motors, Ford Motor Company, Chrysler Corporation, Sears, and other blue-chip U.S.-firms, put their names on foreign-made products.

The author of this introduction purchased an AT&T computer several years ago under the misunderstanding that it was American made. It turns out that the computer was made in Italy by Olivetti and that AT&T put its label on it. The AT&T logo is in a prominent position while "Made in Italy" is in small print on the bottom of the keyboard and on the back of the computer, two places most people do not look. Inside the computer (which most people never see) is a label on the disk drives that states "Toshiba, Made in Japan."

This book will help you determine which products are made in the United States. But this book can only serve as a guide since millions of products are manufactured in the world and only a few hundred can be listed in this book.

The Harm that the Trade Deficit Causes

The United States is experiencing the largest trade deficits in the history of the world. Because we export less than we import our trade deficit is about 100 billion dollars per year. This weakens the United States economy, costs jobs and helps to make the United States the largest debtor nation in the world.

We are buying automobiles, VCRs and other depreciating assets from overseas. Then, with the profits from these sales, the Japanese, Koreans and Europeans are buying our real estate in Los Angeles, Hawaii, New York City and in other major markets. Real estate is an appreciating asset.

Since we are buying depreciating assets overseas, we

must continually replenish them every year. And every year countries with trade surpluses turn those sales into American real property. South Koreans have recently entered the U.S. real estate market with billions of recycled U.S. dollars. In the long run, if trade deficits continue, foreign interests will own most of our real estate. Already 64 percent of the downtown real estate in Los Angeles, 39 percent in Houston and 33 percent in Minneapolis is foreign-owned.

What You Can Do to Help America

By shopping wisely and buying American products consumers can help keep the U.S. economy strong. Buying American helps to keep manufacturing jobs in the United States, it reduces the trade deficit and it helps reduce the transfer of American assets abroad.

The most important purchase that you make is an automobile. Contrary to popular belief, an American automobile will probably cost you less than a comparable car from overseas. Further, it will probably cost you less to repair an American car, over the long run, than an import.

Almost one-half of the trade deficit consists of payments for oil imports. If you conserve energy at home you strengthen the U.S. economy. If you buy a fuel efficient American car you strengthen the United States. For this reason we have not recommended the purchase of U.S.-made gas guzzlers.

In many areas American products appear to be more expensive than overseas competition. However, in general, American-made products are better made and last longer than many imports. Do you remember ever having a problem with a U.S.-made telephone? For example, American-made apparel fits better, wears better and is more colorfast than most imports. A shirt made in Hong Kong may appear cheaper initially, but you (and your country) will pay for it in the long run. According to the International Fabricare Institute the vast majority of the problems with drycleaning are caused by inferior foreign fabrics and dyes.

When You Buy American You are Purchasing Freedom, Environmental Quality and Health and Safety

Included in every U.S.-made product is the cost of providing for the safety and health of American workers. Also included in the price of every American product is the cost of complying with U.S. environmental laws.

But perhaps most import of all, when you buy U.S.-made goods you are showing your support for the most free society and economy in the world. Many goods made in China are made in prison camps, often by political prisoners. The profits are paid to Chinese politicians.

Checklist for Shopping American

This book does not review every type of product on the market. You must learn how to shop, always looking for and reading labels and tags. Here is a short checklist for shopping American:

● **Find and read the label** (all imported products must state country of origin on the product); you may have to turn the product upside down—don't be shy—If a salesman asks what you are doing, tell him you are looking for a made in the USA product label;

● If you can't find U.S.-products at one retailer, go to another;

● If you still can't find an American-made product call the Made in the USA Foundation at (800) USA-PRIDE, and the Foundation will help you find the product that you are looking for.

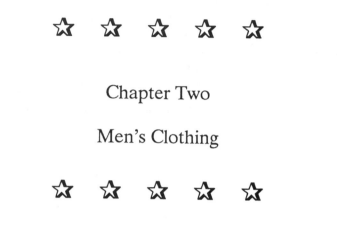

Chapter Two

Men's Clothing

President George Washington insisted that his inaugural suit was made in the U.S.A. In the two hundred years since the first president America has developed its distinct style and fashion. Levi Strauss invented blue jeans in 1853 and "Levi's" are still synonymous with jeans around the world. American clothing is extremely diverse from blue jeans and cowboy boots on one end, to the Tuxedo and Stetson hat on the other.

Many clothing stores do not carry a wide selection of American-made clothing. The following retailers and catalogs carry a good selection of American mens' clothing (in alphabetical order):

L.L. Bean
Brooks Brothers
K-Mart
Kuppenheimer
Lands' End
J.C. Penney
Richmond Brothers
Sears
Wal-Mart

Almost every store that we surveyed stocked some American-made clothing. We surveyed hundreds of stores, including Macys, Bloomingdales, K-Mart, Sears, J.C. Penney, Saks Fifth Avenue, Wal-Mart, Montgomery Ward, Brooks Brothers and Lord & Taylor.

It is easier to find men's clothing that is made in the United States than women's. Hart Shaffner & Marx, a diverse manufacturer of men's suits, has acquired many local chains of men's clothing stores, and every one of them stocks a wide selection of American-made clothing. Gov. Michael Dukakis wore Hart Schaffner and Marx suits during the 1988 Presidential campaign. These stores include Wallachs, Raleighs, Baskin, Silverwoods, Hastings, Jas. K. Wilson, Zachry, Leopold, Price & Rolle, Anton's, Wolf Brothers, Klopfenstein's, Walker's, Porter-Stevens, Hanny's, Liemandt's, Field Bros., Peer Gordon and Kleinhans. These stores carry a wide price range of men's clothing, from top-of-the-line Oxxford suits and sport coats to modestly priced clothing.

Suits and Sport Coats

Oxxford suits and sport jackets are almost universally considered to be the best-made American tailored clothing. Their prices are in the stratosphere as well. Oxxford suits cost $1,000 or more and sport coats are in the $800 range. In addition to the stores listed above these excellent products are available at Neiman-Marcus stores. Chicago-based Oxxford does no advertising and their reputation has spread by word-of-mouth.

Brooks Brothers has stores in major U.S. cities and offers its clothing by catalog. To get a catalog call (800) 274-1815. Brooks Brothers clothing is "preppy"; Suits are in the $300-$600 range. The traditional Brooksgate blazer sells for $250.

European Styling, Made in the USA

Much European-style men's clothing is made in the United States. Such renowned European fashions as Austin-Reed, Burberry's, Ungaro of Paris and Christian Dior have many of their suits and sport coats manufactured in the U.S.

Henry Grethel, although an American designer, calls his clothing line "international." If you like the European look in clothing try on a Henry Grethel suit or sports jacket.

TFW produces a line of casual clothing with a European cachet. TFW features jacket/vests with a pleated, baggy look.

Henry Grethel shirt and tie pictured above.

TFW casual "suit" shown above.

Perry Ellis is another American design house which produces "international" style. Perry Ellis tailored clothing is made in the U.S., but most of his shirts are imported. **Stanley Blacker** sport coats also have an international look, but are less expensive than Perry Ellis designs.

Mid-Range Suits and Sport Coats

Usually less expensive than the suits listed above, but still top-quality, include Hickey-Freeman, Atwood, Joseph Abood, Pferris, Haspel, Palm Beach, Hart Schaffner & Marx and Halston.

Inexpensive Suits and Sport Coats

Richmond Brothers and Kuppenheimer sell suits under their own labels in stores around the country. You can find a good quality suit in these stores for $175 and a sport coat for $100. You will find suits and sport coats in this price range at J.C. Penney, Wal-Mart and K-Mart.

Men's Shirts

Eagle has been manufacturing men's shirts in the United States since 1867 and still makes a top-quality shirt. Hathaway, Christian Dior and Burberry dress shirts are made in the U.S. Most department stores have their own label shirts made in the United States.

Hart Schaffner & Marx suit is shown above.

Blue Jeans

Make sure that you check labels when buying blue jeans. While most are made in America, many are not. The following are made in the USA:

Calvin Klein
Expressions
Levi's
L.L. Bean
Lee
Gap
Power Blues
Rustler (from Wrangler)
Weekend Jeans (J.C. Penney)
Wrangler

Men's Casual Clothing

Made in the USA cotton "polo" shirts are carried in most stores. Designers, including Calvin Klein and Ralph Lauren make most of their polo shirts in the U.S.A. Check the labels. You can find this type of casual shirt at the Gap, Bloomingdales, Macys, Saks Fifth Avenue and many other stores. L.L. Bean has a complete line of polo shirts for about $21 available by mail order. You can request a free catalog by calling (800) 221-4221. Brooks Brothers also sells polo-style shirts ($32) by mail (800) 274-1815.

Lee denim jacket and jeans are pictured above.

Many casual pants are imported. Some Levi's Dockers pants are made in the U.S. as are some Brittania pants. Brooks Brothers and L.L. Bean has wide selections of American-made casual slacks in cotton, wool and corduroy. The Land's End catalog also has quite a few types of made-in-the-USA pants, and an even longer selection of casual shirts. To get their catalog call (800) 356-4444. One brand that sounds American, Bugle Boy, imports most of their line.

Many men's sweaters are imported. American sweaters can be found at L.L. Beans and Brooks Brothers. **Crossings** makes sweaters for men in the U.S. Their all-cotton sweaters are colorful and stylish.

A relatively new company in North Carolina, **Ruff Hewn,** makes high-quality men's casual clothing, including pants and shirts. Their slacks are a notch above jeans in terms of dressiness, but are just as durable. Their clothing is "outdoor-style." To find a store which carries Ruff Hewn clothing call (800) 334-8716.

Henry Grethel also makes a line of casual clothing, including sweaters, slacks and outdoor jackets. Some clothing in this line is imported so watch labels carefully.

The A-2 leather flight jacket was worn by American pilots during World War II. **Cooper Sportswear** was an original supplier of these jackets to the U.S. Air Force. Forty-five years after their retirement these jackets are again official clothing for the Air Force. The jackets ($250) are only available by telephone and mail from MBI Flight Gear, (800) 367-4534, or by joining the U.S. Air Force.

Ruff Hewn clothing is featured in the photograph.

Henry Grethel sweater, turtleneck and jacket are show.

☆ ☆ ☆ ☆ ☆

Chapter Three

Women's Clothing

☆ ☆ ☆ ☆ ☆

Womens clothing is more difficult to nail down than men's clothing: it is a constantly moving target with styles changing every season. Women have to watch their labels more carefully than men because a single designer switches countries more quickly than the fashions themselves. According to our point of view, the women's most disappointing designers are Anne Klein, Donna Karan, Ellen Tracy, Adrienne Vittadini, Chaus, Merona and Liz Claiborne. Liz Claiborne is especially disappointing, because her clothes are everywhere, and because her firm apparently makes no effort to make clothing in the United States. Even her jeans are made in Hong Kong and Singapore. Claiborne's "Great American Collectibles" are made in Hong Kong, Taiwan and Australia.

Women's Suits

Generally, the more expensive the clothing item the more likely that you can find one made in the United States. For example, an inexpensive suit is most likely to be made outside the U.S. in places like Korea and Taiwan. This holds true for both women's suits and coats. The following designers make quality women's suits in the U.S.: **Ralph Lauren, Jones N.Y., Evan Picone, Shelli Segal, Paul Stanley, Bert Newman, Christian Dior, Noviello-Bloom, Georges Marciano, Saville, E.R. Gerard, Nicole Miller, Albert Nipon** (he's an American) and **Gianni Sport.** You can also find high-quality (and expensive) women's suits at **Brooks Brothers.** J.C. Penney carries moderately-priced **Alicia** suits.

Blouses

Evan Picone, Carole Little, Shelli Segal, Finity, Gianni Sport, Georges Marciano, Worthington (J.C. Penney), Sag Harbor, Calvin Klein, L.L. Bean and **Brooks Brothers** make blouses in the USA.

Women's Coats

We criticized Anne Klein earlier, but she makes many fine coats in the U.S. Other designers manufacturing women's coats in America include **Perry Ellis, Christian Dior, Calvin Klein, Evan-Picone, Fashions by Jill, Karen, Tahari, Bicci, Jones New York** and **J.G. Hook.** Carole Cohen's **Drizzle** line includes trend-setting rainwear. **Liz Callahan's Weather Wear** is all made in the U.S. **The Limited** produces one of the best values in women's coats, the Cassidy Coat.

Albert Nipon piped elongated all-wool jacket and skirt.

Calvin Klein pants, sweater and blouse pictured above.

Women's Jeans

The major manufacturers of men's jeans, Levis, Lee and Wrangler also make jeans for women. Other jeans for women include **Ralph Lauren, Calvin Klein, Fetish, Body Blue, Z. Cavaricci, Marithe & Francois Girbaud, Guess, George Marciano, A. Smile** and **L.L. Bean.**

Women's Sweaters

Most women's sweaters are imported, but you can find domestic ones if you look for them. **Finity, Sweater Loft, Calvin Klein, Gap, Lands' End, Norton McNoughton** and **L.L. Bean** produce American-made sweaters. **Beldoch Popper** creates sweaters with matching knit skirts and cardigans. J.C. Penney carries **Across America** sweaters. Montgomery Ward carries **Sheridan Square** sweaters, some of which are made in the U.S.A. K-Mart carries **Ellen D. Kollection** sweaters and **Julie and Delivery, Ltd.** maternity sweaters.

Casual Clothing

Tapemeasure, Azzura, Cotton Hills, Max Studio, Oshkosh, Zero-60 and **Michelle Lamy** produce fine quality casual, cotton-knit outfits, either pants or skirt with a coordinated top. **Z. Cavaricci, Girbaud, Calvin Klein, Palmetto's, Lianne Barnes** and **Georges Marciano** make stylish pants and tops. **Ruff Hewn**, maker of durable, all-American sportswear, is based in High Point, North Carolina. Less expensive women's casual clothing is available at J.C. Penney, K-Mart and Wal-Mart. Top quality traditional casual clothing is available by mail from **L.L. Bean, Lands' End** and **Brooks Brothers.**

Lee "Pepper Stretch" jeans are pictured above.

Guess jeans are pictured above.

Ruff Hewn outfit is shown above.

Formal Wear

Combining style, elegance, and simplicity, **Gunne Sax** has produced numerous lines of dresses and evening wear in the United States.

Conclusion

Look carefully and you will find USA-made women's clothing. If the stores near you do not have what you want, try the mail order firms. Mail order clothing catalogs are required by law to state whether the products are made in America or imported. The law even requires catalogs to specify if the fabric is imported when the garment is sewn in America. Some of the best catalogs for buying American are L.L. Bean (800) 221-4221, Brooks Brothers (800) 274-1815 and Lands' End (800) 356-4444. All three carry complete lines of women's clothing.

☆ ☆ ☆ ☆ ☆

Chapter Four

Children's Clothing

☆ ☆ ☆ ☆ ☆

This is the first year that we included children's clothing in *Made in the USA*. Most department stores, from Nordstrom to Sears, have children's clothing that is made in America. There are several new all-children's chains that have a good selection of American children's clothing: GapKids and Kids R Us. Watch labels because they are the only real indication of what country a garment is made in.

Infants and Toddlers

Three major manufacturers, all producing clothing in the United States, make good quality infantware. They are Oshkosh, Carters and Healthtex. They are available in most stores that carry infant clothing. The other infant clothing available is either very expensive clothing from Europe (France in particular) or very cheap clothing from the Far East. If you cannot afford new American clothing there is nothing wrong with purchasing clothing from a second-hand store, or borrowing clothing from a friend or relative.

Casual Children's Clothing

With children's clothing you must watch labels carefully. One pair of Levi's jeans may be made in the USA and another imported. The following companies manufacture <u>most</u> of their children's clothing in the United States: (in alphabetical order)

Body Glove
Bullfrog
Cherokee
Everlast
Gap Kids
Gotcha
Instinct
Kaynee
Kozmik
L.A. Movers
Lees
Ocean Pacific
Pacific Coast Highway
Palmetto's
Russell
Strike Four
Surfers Alliance
TFW
Zonk

On the other hand, Cotler and Bugle Boy, two names that sound American, import most of their clothing. Don't confuse Pacific Trail with Ocean Pacific or Pacific Coast Highway. Pacific Trail would be more accurately named if it was tagged "Pacific Rim," the home of Hong Kong, Taiwan, Singapore and China. Neighborhood Kids Club clothing is not made in a neighborhood in the United States.

Bullfrog makes casual clothing for boys and girls.

Children mainly wear two types of clothing, casual and very casual. Very casual clothing includes Ocean Pacific, Pacific Coast Highway, Surfers Alliance shorts and tops and athletic wear by Russell and Everlast. Girls should try out L.A. Movers clothing, which is stretch wear made out of DuPont's lycra. All L.A. Movers clothing is made in the USA. Bodygloves also makes girls actionwear.

Ocean Pacific casual fashions shown above.

Jeans are casual clothing for kids, though some children consider it dressing up when they wear them. GapKids and Lee jeans are made in the USA. Jeans by Guess, Levis and other companies are <u>sometimes</u> made in the United States, so watch labels carefully.

TFW KIDZ produces clothing that fills the gap between jeans and dressing up with a sport coat or a dress. They make stylish corduroy pants for boys and girls and cardigan sweaters.

L.A. Movers makes exercise and casual clothing for girls. (Don't confuse this label with "L.A. Gear," which is strictly imported.)

Strike Four clothes are pictured above.

Lee Jeans are featured in the above photograph.

TFW KIDZ boys and girls clothing a shown above.

Dress Clothing for Children

Kids, especially boys, usually hate to get dressed up. TFW makes getting dressed up more stylish, and their clothing is moderately priced. Gant and Firenza also make dress clothing for boys in the USA. Girls skirts and dresses by Emily Rose and Sarah Kent are made in America.

TFW BOYZ jacket ($57) and trousers ($26) have a "European look," with American fit, quality and price.

☆　☆　☆　☆　☆

Chapter Five

Shoes

☆　☆　☆　☆　☆

The United States leads the world in the design of athletic and walking shoes. While other nations are known for the style of their shoes American shoes are designed for comfort, wear and performance. A new trend started in New York City in the 1970s: some of the most fashionable women in the world began wearing athletic shoes to work, and then at the office, changed into their stylish, but uncomfortable, shoes. I will start this chapter with a discussion of athletic shoes and will go on to casual shoes and dress shoes.

Before getting to the specifics we list the ten best American shoe manufacturers:

Allen-Edmonds
Dexter

Johnston & Murphy
Joyce Selby Shoes
New Balance
Red Wing Shoes
Sebago
Van's
E.T. Wright
Zodiak

Athletic Shoes

The company at the leading edge of athletic shoe design is the **New Balance Athletic Shoe** company. The company was founded in 1906 and spent its first fifty years producing arch supports and orthopedic shoes. In the mid-1950s New Balance began to work with runners to manufacture custom-made running shoes. In 1972 in Boston, on the day that the fabled Marathon is run, James S. Davis purchased New Balance. Four years later New Balance introduced the M320 running shoe which was named the number one shoe on the market by *Runners World* magazine. New Balance introduced width sizing to athletic shoes and remains the only major manufacturer to provide it.

New Balance's design expertise does not lie in running shoes alone. It manufactures a complete line of basketball, tennis, fitness, hiking and soccer shoes priced from $45 to $160.

New Balance athletic shoes are shown above.

New Balance offers five widths for its running shoes—nearly unheard of in the athletic shoe industry.

New Balance has recently entered the walking shoe market with a product made in the USA: a high quality alternative to Rockport shoes which seem to be an All-American product, but are produced overseas. Most New Balance shoes are made in the USA but some are imports, so you must check labels on the shoes. L.L. Bean carries many New Balance shoes, so if you have trouble finding them in your area you can order by phone from Beans, twenty-four hours a day, at (800) 221-4221.

Vans has been manufacturing canvas tennis shoes in Orange, California for a generation, and quietly exporting them to more than ten countries. Vans are not well-know on the East Coast. You can order direct from the factory at (714) 974-7414. Vans are similar to

Keds, the primary difference being that Vans are American and Keds are imported.

Vans for men are shown above.

Converse and **Adidas** offer a few shoes that are made in the United States. Converse makes two canvas models in the States. The **Jack Purcell** is an older style canvas tennis shoe which offers new technological advances in tennis shoes, but retains a classic style.

Converse also makes the **Chuck Taylor** basketball shoe in the United States. One can see the original intent of this shoe in old basketball clips. Over the last couple of years, "Chucks" have become more of a fashion item. Converse produces the shoe in a variety of colors. Like the Purcell, the Chuck Taylor lacks the advances of modern basketball shoes. "Chucks," however, offer a fashionable shoe that is relatively inexpensive compared to the higher priced, imported basketball shoes of Nike, Reebok, LA Gear and even Converse's own imported basketball shoes.

Adidas makes several of its tennis shoes in the United States. The **Magnum** and **Stan Smith** for both men and women are made in America. The Stan Smith has, like the Chuck Taylor, accepted a role as a fashion item as much as a tennis shoe. The plain styling of the Stan Smith makes it appealing to those who desire a simple, functional shoe.

Adidas also makes its soccer shoe, the Samba, in the United States.

Men's Dress Shoes

Allen-Edmonds makes the finest men's shoes in the United States, and some say, in the world. Allen-Edmonds Shoe Corporation, based in Wisconsin for more than 50 years, exports its expensive shoes to 33 countries. President George Bush wears these comfortable and classic men's shoes. Nordstrom carries Allen-Edmonds shoes, which sell for from $150 and up. In 1989 Allen-Edmonds added a women's shoe division.

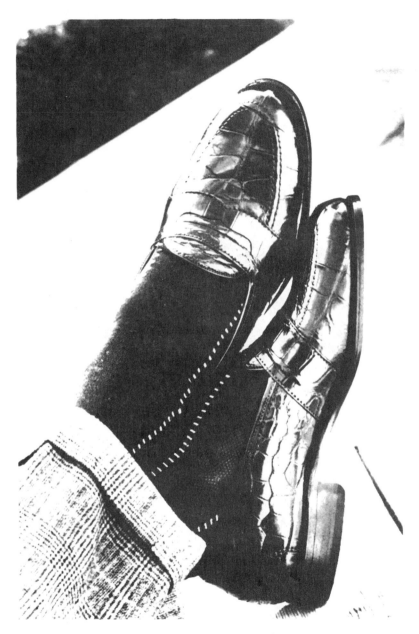

Allen-Edmunds loafers are shown above.

Florsheim still makes some very fine, classic men's dress shoes in the United States, although it imports many of its other shoes.

E.T. Wright manufactures excellent men's dress and casual shoes. If you have trouble finding them, call the Executive Shoe Company at (800) 343-1022 for a catalog. Executive Shoes also carries New Balance and **Sebago shoes**.

Don't forget to put your high-quality shoes in U.S.-made shoe trees like the **Rochester Shoe Tree** or the **Woodlore Shoe Tree** made by Allen-Edmonds.

Johnston & Murphy's "Georgetown II" is shown above.

Johnston & Murphy, based in Nashville, Tennessee, is the oldest shoe manufacturer in the USA, established in 1850. Its shoes are high-quality, hand-made shoes, but are less expensive than Allen-Edmonds.

Casual Men's Shoes

A personal favorite American shoe company is **Zodiac** of Rochester, New Hampshire. Zodiak manufactures both men's and women's shoes: they are comfortable, stylish and off-beat.

Zodiak's "Warning" is pictured above.

More traditional men's shoes are made by **Bass, Bostonian, Hanover** and **Timberland**. One of America's leading shoe manufacturers is **Dexter Shoe Company** of Dexter, Maine. Dexter manufactures a wide-range of value-priced shoes. They are crafted with quality leathers using welt, handsewn and cement construction. Dexter shoes hold up very well (I am wearing a pair now). Dexter exports its products to 29 countries.

Timberland provides an outdoor, rugged look that is both fashionable and functional. Though often expensive, Timberland shoes are worth the cost in terms of durability. Bass, Dexter and Sebago also produce shoes along the same line as Timberland at a lesser price.

In 1946 the **Sebago** shoe company was formed in Maine. Sebago's classic loafer has attained world-wide acceptance; it is sold in 50 countries.

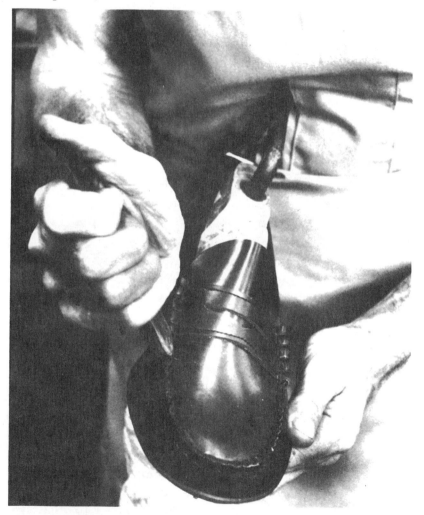

A craftsman is shown making a pair of Sebagos.

Recently, Rockport shoes have become the rage. This shoe has a distinctly rugged, plain, American look. The style can be misleading. Rockport imports all of its shoes.

There are, however, several American companies that provide quality alternatives to Rockport. Both Dexter and **Red Wing** make shoes with the same simple style and comfort of Rockport. Red Wing has a new line of shoes called **Dunoons**. Dunoons cover wider range of styles than Rockport. From casual to sporty to dressy, Red Wing has provided a complete line of shoes that maintains the qualities that make Rockport attractive to consumers. This includes light-weight, ventilated, supportive shoes. Dexter has also adapted this style to its shoes.

Red Wing and Timberland also make heavy-duty boots in the USA. Both produce boots with steel toes for construction and other hazardous work. Each of these companies has a commitment to producing high quality products in the United States.

The **Weinbrenner Shoe Company** of Wisconsin calls itself "The Craftsmen of the Northwoods." Weinbrenner might also be called the "Craftsmen of the Streets and Suburbs." Weinbrenner makes shoes for letter carriers, medical workers, carpenters and other industrial laborers. Weinbrenner's Thorogood line of shoes for law enforcement, postal, fire, safety and emergency related jobs are sturdy shoes. Thorogood shoes are designed for comfort in demanding situations and performance on the job. Weinbrenner also makes the Wood n' Stream line of boots. These boots are primarily for jobs that are outdoors, but Wood n' Stream also makes boots for leisure including the "Ultimate Wading Shoe" designed by Gary Borger.

If you can't find casual men's shoes by these manufacturers, L.L. Bean, in its catalog, offers a good line of
sturdy, well-made shoes, made for Bean's.

Women's Shoes

Quality men's shoes that are made in the USA are
relatively easy to find. This is not true with women's
shoes. Very few pairs of heals are made in the United
States. The major national manufacturer of women's
dress shoes is Joyce Selby, whose shoes can be found
across the country. Selby makes "comfort-flex" shoes
which are dressy, yet walkable, unlike countless
imported shoes, which look great, but are
uncomfortable. To find the nearest Joyce Selby shoe
store call (800) 252-SHOE.

Selby shoes are pictured above.

Selby has been an American manufacturer of shoes for 112 years. Selby shoes are targeted for women who desire a sophisticated, classic style. Selby combines high quality with fashionable creations. This company is noted for excellent fitting qualities, which includes a broad assortment of sizes and widths. Not only has Selby achieved success in the United States, but the company also exports to Europe.

U.S. Shoe also makes Joyce shoes which are geared for a younger set than Selby. These shoes maintain the same quality that is a trademark of Selby. U.S. Shoe has recently introduced **Leslie Fay Footwear**, which is sold primarily through department stores for about $60 to $70 a pair.

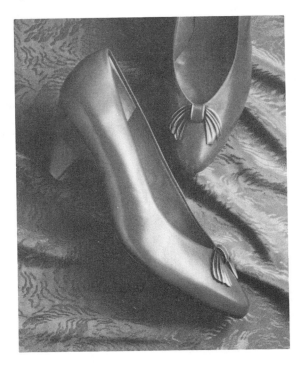

Leslie Fay shoes are shown above.

Cobbies are also made by U.S. Shoe. Cobbies are for younger or more active women. Cobbies makes not only dressy and casual shoes, but also a line of shoes for recreation. These shoes are called **Easy Spirit** and are designed for all active women. Cobbies has recently designed an Easy Spirit shoe that has the inside of an athletic shoe with a dress and casual exterior. It is similar to a Rockport-style shoe for women. Not all Easy Spirit shoes are made in the USA, so be careful.

U.S. Shoe also makes **Capezio** shoes. Capezio are stylish dress heals, some of which are dyable fabric shoes. **Colorifics** specializes in dyable shoes, most of which come in a white fabric which is made to be dyed. Colorifics retailers can be located by calling (800) 225-5746.

Capezio shoes may look Italian but they are not.

U.S. Shoes also has the Red Cross subsidiary which makes practical shoes for nursing and other occupations, as well as for just plain walking. Red Cross is not primarily concerned with fashion, only comfort and function.

The common denominator for all these U.S. Shoe companies is that comfort and fit is combined with fashion for a high quality shoe.

Naturalizer shoes by the Brown Shoe Company are another line of casual women's shoes. They also manufacture **Natural Sport** shoes, which are a comfortable athletic shoe.

Vans manufactures colorful sports/deck shoes for women. To find a Vans retailer near you call (714) 974-7414.

Vans for women are shown above.

Allen-Edmonds (discussed above under men's dress shoes) now makes quality women's shoes. These shoes are "classic" dress shoes which never go out of style.

New Balance athletic shoes come in many styles for women. You will find a better fit than other athletic shoes because each size comes in five or six widths.

Most of the manufacturers of men's casual shoes, such as Dexter, Timberland, Bass and Sebago make similar shoes for women. L.L. Bean also makes hiking and casual women's shoes.

Zodiak shoes and boots are stylish, contemporary and sometimes unusual.

Zodiak boots are pictured above.

Ladies, its time to give up your uncomfortable foreign shoes for a new pair of walking shoes by New

Balance or a pair of Vans. Statistics demonstrate that women buy three times as many pairs of shoes as men, but only wear one pair at a time. Next time that you are shopping buy a pair for yourself. Do your feet a favor and buy state-of-the-art comfort, American-style.

Children's Shoes

Children's shoes are a disaster area for American-made products. American companies, Nike, Reebok and L.A. Gear, import nearly all of their shoes and advertise them to death. Combined with this children rarely wear leather dress or casual shoes. These factors have combined to decimate the children's shoe industry in the United States.

Concerning athletic-type shoes we recommend Vans. Vans makes both tie and velcro shoes for children, both high and low top varieties.

Style 44, 95, 98

A variety of Vans shoes for children are shown above.

Willits of Halifax, PA makes leather childrens shoes

for boys and girls. You can locate a Willits dealer by calling (800) 544-3633. Sebago makes a complete line of boys and girls penny loafers and boat shoes.

Sebago shoes are shown above.

Stride Rite makes <u>some</u> of its shoes in the United States. **Kepner-Scott** of Pennsylvania makes girls leather shoes. Kepner-Scott can be reached at (717) 366-0229. The **Minnetonka Mocassin** company produces children's mocassins. A Minnetonka dealer can be located by calling (612) 331-8493.

☆ ☆ ☆ ☆ ☆

Chapter Six

Bicycles

☆ ☆ ☆ ☆ ☆

Bicycling is one of the most popular sports in the United States. In fact, the number of bicycles sold in the USA has increased by three million per year from 1982 to 1989. The total number of bicycle users in the USA has increased by 16 million, to 88 million in the last six years. However, many of those sales have gone overseas. For example, Sears, the nation's largest retailer carries only imported bicycles, some under the Spalding name.

The bicycle market is complex because it includes everything from children's bikes to racing machines which cost $3,000 or more. The U.S. has quality bicycle manufacturers at the bottom end, at the top end and in between. One American bicycle manufacturer (**Huffy**) produces bicycles in all price ranges.

U.S: World's Most Efficient Manufacturer

The world's most efficient producer of bicycles is located in the USA. **Huffy Corporation,** in addition to being the nation's largest manufacturer, can produce a bike with only 45 minutes of direct labor. This is one-third to one quarter the time needed by the Taiwanese. For example, today 1,700 Huffy employees produce 15,000 bicycles; whereas, ten years ago it took 2,100 employees to produce 10,000 bicycles per day.

Huffy manufactures a complete range of bicycles, from children's models and all-terrain bikes, to world-class racing machines. Huffy bicycles are available at K-Mart, Toys-R-Us, Childworld, Children's Palace, Lionel Kiddy City and through the Sears catalog.

Huffy bikes are produced using mostly American parts, and are all assembled in Ohio. Huffy produces bicycles in nearly every category from beginners to touring bicycles for adults. Most of Huffy's products still carry suggested retail prices below $150. The company's childrens bicycles are even more affordable with most retailing for under $100. The company also sells several more expensive BMX (Bicycle MotoCross) and ATB models for teenagers. Finally, Huffy does produce a complete line of ten speeds, touring and mountain bikes targeted towards adults.

Although Huffy's position as a mass market retailer has caused many to belittle the quality of their products, this reputation is not accurate. Huffy was selected by the U.S. Cycling Federation to be the bike of the National Team. The American bicycles for the 1984 Olympics were designed at Huffy's Technical Development Center in Dayton, Ohio. At the Olympics in Los Angeles that year Americans won five of their nine medals atop Huffy-designed bicycles.

The technical innovation needed to win at the Olympics has filtered down to Huffy's mass production models. The disc wheels that are featured on Huffy's **Targa** and **Exterminator** models were first seen in the Olympic games.

A Huffy Black Bear All-Terrain Bike is shown above.

Another large manufacturer of bikes in the USA is **Murray**, whose bicycles are marketed at J.C. Penney, K-Mart, Toy-R-Us, Wal-Mart and other retailers. All of Murray's bikes retail in the United States for under $150. Murray bicycles are assembled in the USA using mainly American parts. At one time the company tried moving its manufacturing operations abroad, but found they could produce a better bike more efficiently in the United States.

Columbia and **Roadmaster** manufacture modestly priced bicycles in the U.S. **Schwinn** and **Raleigh** produce higher price bicycles in America and import lower-priced bicycles.

Mountain Bicycles

In addition to being among the most efficient mass market producers of bicycles the USA also leads the field in the development of Mountain or All-Terrain Bicycles. The first production ATB anywhere was made in the USA by the **Specialized Bike Co.** of California. All of Specialized bikes are now made abroad, except for two models. The company manufactures two very expensive bikes here in the United States: the **Stump-jumper Epic** and the **Allez Epic.**

State-of-the-art bicycle manufacturing and aircraft construction share some common skills. Both attempt to make the strongest frame possible at the lightest weight. Because of this both use advanced materials technology to combine titanium, aluminum, exotic steels, chrome/molybdenum and carbon-fiber into frames. Huffy manufactures a carbon-fiber bicycle which weighs 14 pounds. The price is from $8,000 to $10,000, a bargain compared to the Stealth bomber made out of the same materials. Some smaller bicycle manufacturers use aircraft technology to produce light-weight metal frames and ultralight carbon-fiber frames, including:

> **Cannondale Bicycles** (Bedford, PA)
> **Fat City Bicycle Co.,** (Somerville, MA)
> **Haro Bicycles,** (Carlsbad, CA)
> **Kestrel** (Watsonville, CA)
> **Klein Bicycle Co.** (Chehalis, WA)
> **Manitou,** (Colorado Springs, CO)

Marin Mountain Bike Co., (Marin County, CA)
Ritchey, (Redwood City, CA)
Serotta Bicycles, (Middle Grove, NY)
Titan, Inc, (Eugene, OR)
Yeti Bicycles, (Agoura Hills, CA)

Trek Manufacturing is another bicycle company which makes some of its frames here in the United States. All Trek Series 900 frames are made here in America, while all the Series 800 bikes are manufactured in Taiwan. Trek bikes, like many of the American bicycles, are directed towards the serious rider; prices for the American manufactured Trek bikes start at $500 and up.

Cannondale manufactures sophisticated high performance ATBs and touring bikes. The company was at the vanguard of the aluminum bike revolution; today they are still regarded as one of the innovators in the bicycle industry.

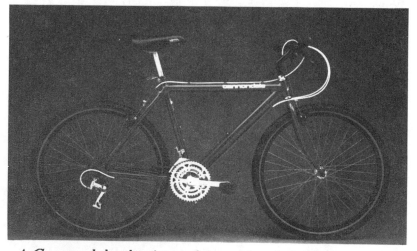

A Cannondale aluminum-frame bicycle is shown.

Cannondale manufactures its frames in the USA, but like all bike companies many of its components are imported. Although Cannondale did not start manufacturing its first bike until 1983 it now commands a significant share of the higher priced end of the market.

Cannondale, which introduced the first affordably priced all-aluminum frame seven years ago, manufactures and assembles all its bikes at the company's Bedford, Pennsylvania plant. The company is currently planning to open another Pennsylvania factory soon due to the increased demand for Cannondale products. In a twist on the usual story, Cannondale is now exporting its products to the Far East. Cannondale has just introduced Elevated Suspension Technology (ETS), which provides a better riding bicycle.

In the field of ATB design, America is generally acknowledged to be the leader. No matter where an American company chooses to have its bikes manufactured, all the design work is done here in the USA. As the originator of the mountain bike, most experts agree that the rest of the world looks to the USA for advances in design and technology. Even though bike experts will agree that the Japanese designed ATBs are better now than they were, all the most respected bike designers, and small bike workshops producing advanced ATBs are located in the USA.

A Klein aluminum bicycle is shown above.

Gary Klein is regarded as one of the top designers of aluminum-frame bicycles. His bikes are exported to 23 countries. Prices start at $1125 but average $1,400-$1,500, depending on the components ordered.

Chris Chance of Fat City Cycles prefers to make his

bicycles out of steel. Every joint on a Fat City cycle is plasma welded, a unique process that puts Fat City on the cutting edge of technology. Fat City cycles are mostly seen in the Boston area, but keep your eye out for them elsewhere. Chris Chance has been tinkering with bicycle geometry to make a better riding vehicle and many bicycle magazines believe that he has.

Haro Designs produces both aluminum and steel alloy bicycle frames. Haro has also been modifying frame geometrics to make an easier riding bicycle.

Titan manufactures titanium frame bicycles. Titanium is used in aircraft frames and is lighter and stronger than aluminum. The frames alone sell for about $1,000 and up. Titan also produces BMX bikes out of Chrome-Molybdenum, starting at about $200.

Kestrel frames are made out of graphite fibers and kevlar. The frames alone are also more than $1,000. Kestrel frames are distributed by Schwinn and can be ordered from any Schwinn dealer.

Components

I have heard the complaints that "all bicycle components are imported." In truth you can buy made-in-the-USA components for every part of a bicycle except two: tires and deraileur. **Sun Chinook** makes rims and spokes in the U.S. They are available from Titan at (503) 683-8787. Titan makes use of many American- made components.

Bullseye makes state-of-the-art cranks and other components in Burbank, CA. Their light-weight steel

alloy cranks can be ordered by calling (818) 846-9163.
Cook Brothers makes cranks out of aircraft aluminum,
as well as stems, hubs and bottom brackets. Cook Bros.
can be reached in Santa Ana, CA at (714) 835-2700.
Yeti Cycles and Klein make their own aluminum
stems. Gary Helfrich of Arctos Machine, Camp
Meeker, CA, makes ultra-light titanium stems. If I left
out someone, please let me know for next year's book.
In any event, the American bicycle industry is alive
and well, living on the leading edge of bicycle
technology.

Tricycles

Although not technically a bicycle, the tricycle is
usually a child's first cycle. Most tricycles sold in the
United States are imported. One domestic tricycle
worth searching for is the Fisher-Price **Trike**. This
tricycle is rugged, durable and rust-resistant, made
mostly of plastic. The seat lifts up to reveal a storage
compartment which your child will stuff with rocks,
junk and other personal items. The trike sells for about
$30.

☆　☆　☆　☆　☆

Chapter Seven

Motorcycles: Harley-Davidson

An American Classic

☆　☆　☆　☆　☆

"Get your motor runnin'/ Headin' out on the highway/ Looking for Adventure."

Nothing better exemplifies that uniquely American spirit than those lines from *Easy Rider*. What was Peter Fonda's motorcycle of choice in that classic film? Harley-Davidson, of course. Harley is the last All-American manufacturer of motorcycles. At one time more than 300 U.S. companies produced motorcycles.

Today, **Harley-Davidson** manufactures twenty-one different models in four factories in the United States. Harley motorcycles are known for their classic styling combined with the best of modern computer-aided design technology.

Beginning in the early eighties Harley-Davidson completely overhauled its design and manufacturing operations. The company improved the quality of their motorcycles through engine technology improvements, design advances and new organizational techniques.

The changes Harley-Davidson initiated included the development of a new engine, the V2 Evolution, which is the mainstay of the Harley line. In addition, the company also improved the gearbox and engine mounting which reduced vibration and made for a smoother ride. These improvements allowed Harley-Davidson to decrease manufacturing costs and production time, while dramatically increasing quality and reliability. When the quality and reliability of Harleys began to improve, sales mounted a steady climb upward.

Harley-Davidson has the most loyal customers in the business, thanks in part to the strong support the company offers to every customer. This includes a free membership the first year in the Harley Owners Group (H.O.G.), the national club for Harley-Davidson afficiandos. Of course Harley-Davidson motorcycles are better than 95 percent manufactured with American parts. The company also exports to Japan, Australia, Europe and the Persian Gulf, with Japan being one of Harley-Davidson's fastest growing new markets. As Malcolm Forbes has pointed out, the real tribute to Harley-Davidson comes when one realizes that their motorcycle designs are the most copied in the world.

The Harley Sporter is pictured above.

The legendary **Sportster**, first introduced in 1957, is an excellent example of this. Beneath the classic design and shiny chrome lies a motorcycle as sophisticated as any on the road. In today's world of ultra-technological motorcycles, the Sportster lives up to its heritage by providing "no frills just raw thrills." The Sportster serves as an introduction to Harley-Davidson for many buyers.

The merging of technology and classical design is also seen in Harley's line of touring motorcycles. Harley's touring motorcycles appeal to older, more experienced riders. The average **Touring Series** buyer is the oldest in the Harley product line. The intense loyalty towards Harley-Davidson is also evidenced by the fact that more than 60 percent of Touring Series buyers have already owned at least one Harley already.

The Tour Glide Ultra Classic is shown above.

Harley's touring models are designed with the long trip in mind. All the motorcycles have certain amenities such as self-canceling turn signals, extra comfortable seats, and the ability to add plenty of electrical accessories. Many of the Harley-Davidson tourers can also be equipped with a premium sound system and a CB/intercom system. Harley also offers a sidecar option on some motorcycles in this catergory. Harley-Davidson is currently the only original equipment manufacturer to offer sidecars.

With the continuing success of Harley-Davidson in the eighties the company has added the **FatBoy**, a member of the Softail line, featuring a bold silver on silver design. This motorcycle includes custom metal fenders, shotgun style dual exhausts, and textured leather seat. However, beneath the classic styling is a technologically advanced motorcycle equipped with the Evolutionary V2 engine.

Japanese Motorcycles Made in America

Harley-Davidson may be the only American company still manufacturing cycles in the USA, but it still ranks only fifth in total sales with 9.4 percent of the market; an increase from 3.3 percent only five years ago. Harley-Davidson is the dominant force in the large motorcycle market. The company controls nearly fifty percent of the market for motorcycles 850 cc or larger. Harley, surprisingly, has not entered the market for smaller engined or off-road motorcycles. However, given the company's overall success, it seems reasonable that Harley-Davidson could produce a competitive bike in these categories. The top four companies selling motorcycles in the American market are all foreign: Honda, Yamaha, Suzuki and Kawasaki. Honda and Kawasaki are the only two of these companies manufacturing motorcycles in the United States.

Honda maintains a plant in Marysville, Ohio where all motorcycles over 750 cc sold in the USA are made. Honda imports smaller bikes from Japan. Honda estimates that about two-fifths of the motorcycles it sells in the USA are made at the Marysville plant. One reason for this dichotomy is that Japanese manufacturers have voluntarily, for safety reasons, agreed not to sell motorcycles with engines over 750 cc in Japan. In Japan large bikes are considered dangerous. A number of the bikes Honda makes in the USA are exported to Europe. Honda is presently the number one seller of motorcycles in the USA, claiming almost 40 percent of the American market.

Kawasaki also manufactures motorcycles in the USA, although they have recently reduced production at their plant to increase production of their three and four wheel sport vehicles. Similar to Honda, Kawasaki imports all of its motorcycles with engines smaller than 750 cc.

☆ ☆ ☆ ☆ ☆

Chapter Eight

Best American Cars

☆ ☆ ☆ ☆ ☆

In general American cars are safer, cheaper to operate and less expensive to purchase than foreign automobiles. Because American cars are larger and heavier they fare better in accidents. They are less expensive to maintain because repair parts are more readily available and mechanics specializing in imported cars generally charge more per hour.

Criteria for Selecting the Best Cars

Selecting an automobile is a very complicated process. We used the following criteria (not in order of importance) to make our selections:

☐ Safety
☐ Performance

□ Reliability

□ Design, styling, aerodynamics

□ Fuel efficiency

We did not use a system of awarding a certain number of points for each criteria. We used limitations. For example if a car had very poor gasoline mileage we excluded it from consideration entirely, because oil consumption in the United States is the cause for about half of our trade deficit. Another example is safety: if a car (according to data from the Highway Loss Data Institute, an insurance industry nonprofit association) had 50 percent or more injuries in accidents, or 50 percent more serious injuries, than the average car, the car was considered unacceptable.

American Cars: Safest in the World

No U.S. car was excluded from consideration in this book because of the safety standard. However, twelve foreign cars were unacceptably dangerous according to this objective criteria, and they are (in order of the most dangerous first):

The Dangerous Dozen

1. Hyundai Excel
2. Mitsubishi Precis
3. Geo Metro (formely Chevrolet Sprint)
4. Isuzu I-Mark
5. Geo Storm (formerly Chevrolet Spectrum)
6. Yugo
7. Mitsubishi Mirage (same as Colt)

8. Mitsubishi Cordia
9. Mitsubishi Tredia (now Galant)
10. Nissan Sentra
11. Pontiac LeMans
12. Plymouth/Dodge Colt

The Korean-made Hyundai Excel and its identical twin the Mitsubishi Precis are the most dangerous cars on the American road. According to the Highway Loss Data Institute the Hyundai Excel is 89 percent more dangerous than the average car. It is approximately seventy percent more dangerous than the Plymouth Sundance/Dodge Shadow compact car, yet is comparably priced. If you happen to survive an accident in your Hyundai, your repair bill will be more than thirty percent above that of the Plymouth. Knowing the risks of the Hyundai most consumers would choose a safer car.

Volvo advertises the safety of its cars, but it turns out that the Ford Taurus/Mercury Sable is safer, and less expensive to repair, than the Volvo 240. In fact, the Taurus is superior is styling, aerodynamics, dependability and traction in ice and snow and the only factor that it is lower than the Volvo is price.

Other Criteria

Concerning the other criteria we consulted with the editor of *Car & Driver* magazine, *Consumer Reports*, J.D. Power and Associates and other automotive and consumer experts.

J.D. Power & Associates ranks automobiles according to consumer satisfaction. In their 1989 report, for the first time J.D. Power found that U.S.-manufactured vehicles were superior to European automobiles in quality. This corresponds to our own survey results showing that during the past five years the quality of American automobiles has increased dramatically. The J.D. Power findings are much more impressive when you consider the fact that only the best European cars were compared with all American cars. The reason for this is that most small, inexpensive European cars are not exported to the USA. Peugeot and Volvo, for example, do not sell their small cars in America. Fiat, the largest automaker in Europe, dropped out of the American market because its cars were considered unsafe and inferior, unable to compete in the fiercely competitive U.S. market.

Car and Driver's Top Ten

Car and Driver magazine provided us with their opinion on the best American cars regardless of price. No inexpensive cars were in their top ten selections. We generally agree with them on their choices. Here is *Car and Driver's* list of the ten best American cars (in alphabetical order):

Chevrolet Corvette
Ford Mustang GT
Ford Probe GT
Ford Taurus/SHO Taurus
Ford Thunderbird SC
Honda Accord
Lincoln Continental
Plymouth Laser/Eagle Talon
Plymouth Grand Caravan/Dodge Grand Caravan
Pontiac Bonneville SE

If You Really Think Japanese Cars are Better, Buy One Made in the U.S.A.

In 1990, for the first time, more than one million Japanese cars came off the assembly lines in the United States. We would prefer that you buy a "real" American car, but if you like Japanese cars, by the most American ones that you can get.

Honda was the first Japanese automaker to manufacture vehicles in the U.S. Honda now makes all of its Accord models in Marysville, Ohio (all that are sold in the United States) and some of its Civic models. Hondas made in the U.S. begin their serial numbers with a '1' while those imported from Japan start with a 'J.' Honda exports the Accord Coupe from the U.S. to Japan and Europe and will begin manufacturing an Accord Stationwagon in Ohio 1991. The Accord Stationwagon is the first Honda to be 100 percent designed in the U.S.A. The U.S. content on the Accord models is approximately 75%, which is the magic number that makes it officially an "American" car. Honda engines and transmissions are also made in Ohio.

The Ford Motor Company owns about one-third of Mazda. Mazda has built a large manufacturing facility in Flat Rock, Michigan, where it produces the Ford Probe, the Mazda MX-6 and the Mazda 626. The new Ford Escort is essentially a Mazda 323. The Mazda in made in Japan while the Ford is manufactured in Michigan.

General Motors and Toyota joined forces to form New United Motors, Inc. in Fremont, California, where Toyota Corollas and Geo Prizms are produced. These two cars are identical and were designed by Toyota. Toyota also manufactures some of its popular Camry model in Kentucky. The serial number of Toyotas made in Japan begin with a 'J.' Those made in the United States are equipped with G.M.-produced Delco batteries.

Nissan has begun to manufacture some of its Sentra models in Smyrna, Tennessee. The label on the side of the Sentra will specify where the car was manufactured. Note that this is a very dangerous car.

Chrysler Corporation and Mitsubishi jointly formed the Diamond Star Motor Corporation in Illinois. At this plant virtually identical cars are produced as Plymouth Lasers, Eagle Talons and Mitsubishi Eclipses. The engines in these vehicles were manufactured and designed by Mitsubishi.

If you must have a Japanese car, then consider buying one that is manufactured in the United States. However, before doing so test drive several American cars recommended in this chapter.

Basic Transportion for Under $10,000

If you are considering buying a Toyota Corolla, a Hyundai Excel or a Nissan Sentra (the last two are very dangerous) you should consider the following American alternatives. While the Hyundai may cost you less initially, you will pay for it in terms of higher insurance costs and higher risk of bodily injury.

Dodge Shadow/Plymouth Sundance

These twin economy cars were introduced to the market for the 1987 model year. *Consumer Reports* finds them to be more reliable than the average car, but warns that the turbo version is more prone to need repairs. These are among the safest small cars, with front-wheel drive, and include driver-side airbag. For 1991 the Sundance will be available as a convertible.

The New Ford Escort

Ford totally redesigned its Escort model for 1991, and improved it drastically. Last year we excluded the Escort, because, among other problems, it was a ten-year old design. The new Escort looks alot like the old one but is mechanically superior and is safer. The Escort and the Mazda 323/Protege are based on the same design, the primary difference being that the Escort is made in the U.S.A. The similar-looking Mercury Tracer is made in Mexico. It is interesting to note that the Tracer is not less expensive than the Escort. The Escort also comes as a stationwagon.

Chevrolet Cavalier/Pontiac Sunbird

These virtually identical General Motors' cars offer a good value for the dollar. They are larger and safer than comparably priced imports.

Geo Prizm (formerly the Chevy Nova)

If you really like the Toyota Corolla buy the Prizm instead. The Prizm is virtually identical to the Toyota; Both are manufactured in Fremont, California on the same assembly line. Compare the Prizm to the Cavalier at a Chevrolet/Geo dealer and decide for yourself. The Prizm is recommended by *Consumer Reports.*

Compact Cars from $10,000-$15,000

Saturn

General Motors has launched a new division, the Saturn Corporation, which may rejuvenate the largest auto maker in the world. Saturn has already been issued 16 patents for improvements to auto technology and has 15 patent applications pending. In addition,

Saturn engineers developed the sixth generation of anti-lock brakes which will be used on other GM cars. Disappointingly, these brakes are an option, not standard on the Saturn.

The Saturn is available as either a two or four-door, both pictured above. GM has spent five years developing these cars and the United Auto Workers have been intimately involved in this new car. Give it a test drive.

Ford Tempo/Mercury Topaz

These two cars may cost you a bit over $10,000, although stripped models can be had for under that amount. The Mercury Topaz is better looking than the Tempo, but otherwise the two cars are identical. Both of these cars are available with four-wheel drive for about $1000 extra; otherwise the drive system is front-wheel drive. These cars are fairly safe, comparable to the Olds Calais and Pontiac Grand Am.

Dodge Spirit /Plymouth Acclaim

Both the Spirit, and its virtually identical twin, the Acclaim, were among the first cars to include a driver's-side airbag as standard equipment. These cars are priced below the comparably sized Honda Accord, Toyota Camry and Nissan Stanza, and in independent surveys consumers prefered to Dodge and Plymouth. Both cars are also recommended by *Consumer Reports*.

Oldsmobile Calais/Pontiac Grand Am/Buick Skylark

These three cars are identical under their metal skin, but all give a different appearance. All three can be fitted with a "Quad 4" engine, which is a sixteen-valve, four cylinder engine. This engine will give you the power of a six, or even a small eight, with better fuel efficiency. These cars are fairly safe, comparable to the Tempo and Topaz.

Two-Door Sports Coupes Under $20,000

Honda Accord Coupe

Many people believe that the Honda Accord is made in Japan. Although some Accords are man- ufactured in Japan this sleek two-door coupe is made only in the United States in Marysville, Ohio. In fact Honda plans to export 50,000 Accord Coupes to Japan in 1991. The first Coupes were exported to Japan in 1990 with left-hand drive. In 1991 the export-version coupes will be equiped with right-hand drive (they drive on the left side of the road in Japan). In case you were wondering, the domestic content of this Honda Accord is about 75 percent. Honda was the first Japanese automobile company to begin manufacturing in the United States (1982) and now builds 400,000 cars a year in the U.S. The Honda Accord ranks third on the J.D. Power Consumer Satisfaction Index.

Ford Thunderbird/Mercury Cougar

The Thunderbird is *Motor Trend's* Car of the Year and is on *Car and Driver's* list of the ten best American Cars. In addition *Consumer Reports* recommends these cars. If you like the BMW you will like the Thunderbird at half the BMW price. Like the BMW it is powerful and agile, with rear wheel drive. If you want a front-wheel drive coupe with the styling of a Thunderbird, test-drive a Pontiac Grand Prix (described on the next page).

Pontiac Grand Prix/Oldsmobile Cutlass Supreme /Buick Regal

These sport coupes are the best-looking American coupes to come out of Detroit in a long time. In 1990 they were joined by a very aerodynamic four door, and later in 1990 the Cutlass version was available as a convertible.

Sedans for Under $20,000

Ford Taurus and Mercury Sable

These two cars are recommended by almost everybody, including *Consumer Reports* and *Car and Driver*. In addition according to the Highway Loss Data Institute the Taurus is one of the safest sedans on the market, even safer than the highly-touted Volvo 244. These cars have front-wheel drive. A special Taurus SHO model is equipped with a 24-valve V-6 engine.

Chevrolet Lumina

The Lumina is a new Chevrolet model which looks somewhat like the Taurus, is aerodynamic and has front-wheel drive. The Pontiac Grand Prix, the Oldsmobile Cutlass Supreme and the Buick Regal are built on the same chassis and underneath their different sheet metal are virtually identical. Unlike the Taurus, the Lumina is available as a two-door coupe.

Pontiac Bonneville, Buick LeSabre and Olds 88 Royale

Consumer Reports and *Road and Track* recommend the Bonneville SE, which is the sportier edition of the Pontiac. The LeSabre ranks number two on the J.D. Power's New Car Initial Quality Survey, ahead of Mercedes Benz and Toyota. This survey is taken three months after customers take delivery and ranks customer satisfaction/complaints at that time. These cars are very substantial, and very safe. Even though all three cars are virtually identical the Bonneville ranks as the safest and gets the best reviews.

Convertibles Under $20,000

Sundance Convertible

New for 1991 the convertible Sundance is an entry-level convertible, ideal for the young at heart. It is equipped with a driver's side airbag, and should be safer than the Mustang convertible.

Ford Mustang Convertible

The Mustang has remained virtually unchanged for a decade. *Motor Trend* calls it a "best buy," *Car and Driver* and *Consumer Reports* recommend it. I have owned one for four years and have had no problems with it. My only complaint is that, because of its rear-wheel drive, it is poor in snow and ice.

Oldsmobile Cutlass Supreme Convertible

GM only plans to produce 3,000 of these V-6 powered convertibles in 1991. They could probably sell 5 to 10 times that number. Because of their scarcity you will probably pay over $20,000, since most are equipped with all accessories.

Chrysler LeBaron Convertible

This is one of the only convertibles designed to be a convertible, as compared to a "chop job." Many convertibles are manufactured as hardtops and then have their roof cut off. The LeBaron, powered by its front wheels, is more aerodynamic than the Mustang.

Sports Cars

Chevrolet Corvette

Car and Driver considers it to be one of the five best cars in the world. *Consumer Reports* doesn't recommend it because of its high-performance and fiberglass body. But insurance data demonstrates that the Corvette is a very safe car, safer than the Volvo 244, safer than the BMW 300 series. New for 1990 is the Corvette ZR-1, an ultra-high performance sports car, comparable in every way to a Ferrari for half the price. At $58,000 it is the most expensive Corvette ever. The standard Corvette will cost you about $30,000, quite a value compared with Porsche and other European sports cars.

Vector

If you can afford the $250,000 price tag the Vector is one of the fastest cars in the world. Manufactured in California of Kevlar, carbon fibers and epoxy, it is the Stealth bomber of the automotive world. With a 600 horsepower V-8 it has a top speed of more than 200 miles per hour. If you don't have a dealer near you call the factory at 213/522-5500.

(Note: the Vector does not meet our fuel economy standards, but has been included because none of its competitors, Ferrari, Lamborghini and forth, meet the standard either.)

Ford Probe

The Ford Probe is built on the same assembly line in Flat Rock, Michigan as the Mazda MX-6. The Probe is sleeker than the Mazda, but besides sheet metal, the two cars are the same. *Motor Trend, Car and Driver* and *Consumer Reports* recommends the Probe. It is not an "All-American" car because it contains many Mazda parts, but nevertheless, we recommend it.

Plymouth Laser/Eagle Talon Four-Wheel Drive

Both of these cars are built in Illinois at Diamond Star Motors, a joint venture between Mitsubishi and Chrysler. They are four-wheel drive, moderately priced sports cars, which look like they cost twice as much.

Luxury Cars

Lincoln Continental

This is the first American car which compares with Europe's ultra-expensive luxury cars. It is less than half the price of an S-class Mercedes, yet in several ways is a better car. It is a front-wheel drive car, with antilock brakes and a V-6 engine. The interior is leather. The car is a stretched Ford Taurus/Mercury Sable with the leg room of the largest Mercedes, the 560 SEL, which sells for more about $80,000.

Cadillac Allante

Car and Driver found the two-seat Allante to be superior to the Mercedes SL. The only drawback to the Allante is its price—over $50,000. The Allante body in made in Italy by Pininfarina, but the rest of the car is all-American.

Avanti

The Avanti was designed more than 25 years ago by Raymond Loewy, the foremost American industrial designer. The Avanti is the last hand-made American car. It takes 1,000 hours to custom build each Avanti, which is now available as a two-door, four-door and convertible. For about $35,000 the Avanti is a great American value. Its five liter, GM V8 engine can be serviced at any General Motors dealership. For the Avanti dealer nearest you call (216) 740-2821, or (800) 548-6350.

Buick Reatta

If you like the Allante but can't afford it, take a look at the Buick Reatta. It's a two-seater with panache, available in both hardtop and convertible versions for about $25,000.

Four-Wheel Drive Cars

1991 should be a banner year for four-wheel drive American vehicles. Ford introduced its 1991 Explorer in the spring of 1990 and I liked it so much that I bought one. *Four-Wheel Drive* magazine, as well as *Road and Track* and Motor Trend gave it top marks; Chevy new four-door S-10 Blazer came out second best but beats the competition from Japan. I don't know why it took GM and Ford a decade to come out with a four door, four-wheel drive station wagon (truck), but they're finally here.

Jeep Wrangler

You can still buy a Jeep, the classic American off-road vehicle, for under $10,000. *4Wheel & Off Road* and *Four Wheeler* magazines named the Wrangler a "Best Buy."

Ford Explorer

This is the smoothest driving truck or four-wheel drive wagon that I have experienced. It is roomy, comfortable, powerful and well-designed. It even has a change dispenser to keep coins handy for tolls. The Explorer comes with rear antilock brakes and compares favorably with the $40,000 Range Rover.

Chevy S-10 Blazer/GM S-15 Jimmy/Olds Bravada

Newly designed for 1991 the Blazer comes in four door and two-door models, and is about a foot longer than last year. The Blazer comes standard with four-wheel anti-lock brakes. New for 1991 is the Oldsmobile Bravada. The Bravada is identical in sheet metal to the Blazer and GM S-15 Jimmy, but on the interior it is an upscale model.

Jeep Cherokee

Cherokee offers an optional four-wheel anti-lock braking system. The Cherokee is the U.S.'s leading four-door sport utility vehicle. It is available in either full-time four-wheel drive or part-time four wheel drive. The Cherokee is somewhat smaller than the Explorer and the Blazer.

Other Four-Wheel Drive Options

Many other American vehicles now come with four-wheel drive options. They include the new GM mini-vans, including the Pontiac TranSport and the Chevy Lumina APV, the Ford Aerostar minivan, the Plymouth Laser /Eagle Talon and the Ford Tempo.

Minivans and Stationwagons

Plymouth/Dodge Grand Caravan

Chrysler Corporation invented the minivan when it introduced the Plymouth and Dodge Caravans in the early 1980s. In 1988 Chrysler introduced the Grand Caravan, which is about one and one-half feet longer than the standard model. The Grand Caravans have two major advantages over the standard model: the extra room makes trips much more comfortable and the Grand Caravan is made in the United States, while the ordinary caravans are assembled in Canada. *Car and Driver* says that the first minivan has been copied, but that the Chrysler minivans have held up to the competition. Front-wheel drive gives the Grand Caravan traction in snow and ice.

Ford Aerostar

The Ford Aerostar is slightly more aerodynamic than the Caravan models and has rear-wheel drive which some argue improves handling, but with less traction in snow and ice. Aerostar is introducing a four-wheel drive version in 1990 which will make it better in foul whether than any two-wheel propulsion system.

Chevrolet Lumina APV/Pontiac TranSport

The newest competition in the minivan field is from General Motors. It is vast improvement over the early, boxy GM small vans. With a drag coefficient of 0.30 it is more aerodynamic than the Corvette. This is an eye-grabber, with good handling front-wheel drive and plastic body. Before buying any of these three good minivans take them all for a test drive. All of them beat the foreign competition in handling, styling, comfort and price.

Chevrolet Cavalier Station Wagon

This is one of the least expensive small wagons on the market.

Ford Escort Station Wagon

Newly redesigned for 1991 the Escort wagon is the best American small station wagon.

Ford Taurus/Mercury Sable Station Wagon

The looks of the Taurus and Sable wagons take some getting used to, but this is a driver's station wagon. If you drive it you will forget that it is a roomy station wagon. Former Volvo wagon owners will be comforted to know that this front-wheel drive, aerodynamic wagon is <u>safer</u> that the Volvo 245 wagon.

Honda Accord Wagon

The Honda Accord wagon was designed in the United States and manufactured in Marysville, Ohio. It is 75 percent American. The Accord has always ranked as one of the best cars according to J.D. Power and *Consumer Reports.*

Conclusion

We have provided you with more than 30 great American cars. If you are considering buying a foreign car, the following is a list of American alternatives to foreign cars. Before buying any of the foreign cars listed below you owe it to yourself and your country to test drive one or more of the alternatives.

If you long for the days of the 1950s and 1960s when American cars were king of the road **American Dream Cars** will sell you a totally rebuilt 1957

Chevrolet Bel Air, original Ford Mustang, Pontiac GTO or other classic, with new Goodyear tires, a rebuilt engine and transmission, new AM-FM cassette, stainless steel front disc brakes, air conditioning, new windshield, new upholstery and paint. These classics come with a 12-month, bumper-to-bumper warranty, with a 36 month drive train warranty. For more information call American Dream Car at (301) 907-0308.

Foreign Car	American Alternatives
Acura	Ford Taurus/Mercury Sable
Audi	Ford Taurus/Mercury Sable
BMW 325i	Thunderbird/Cougar/LeBaron
BMW 325 Convertible	Mustang/LeBaron Convertible
BMW 500/700 series	Lincoln Continental
Jaguar	Lincoln Continental/Avanti
Lexus, Infiniti	Lincoln Continental/Avanti
Mazda 323	Plymouth Sundance, Ford Escort
Mazda 626	Ford Tempo/Saturn
Mazda RX 7	Corvette/Mustang/Reatta
Mazda 929	Ford Taurus/Mercury Sable
Mercedes 500 SL	Allante, Avanti, Reatta
Mercedes 190/300	Sable, Lincoln Continental
Mercedes S Class	Lincoln Continental
Nissan Sentra	Sundance, Shadow, Cavalier
Nissan Maxima	Taurus, Sable, Cutlass Supreme
Range Rover	Ford Explorer
Toyota Camry	Taurus, Sable, Cutlass Supreme
Toyota Corolla	Geo Prizm, Cavalier, Sundance
Toyota Celica/Supra	Ford Probe, Laser
Toyota Landcruiser	Ford Explorer
Volvo	Taurus, Sable, Lumina

☆　☆　☆　☆　☆

Chapter Nine

Best American Trucks

by Mike Ferrara

☆　☆　☆　☆　☆

There's something inherently friendly about pickup trucks. Despite the ever-changing styling whims of car designers, pickups have managed to keep their familiar look. Although refined through the years, their basic layout—right down to the solid rear axles and leaf springs—still resembles the first pickups introduced in the 1920s. These light trucks also feel good because their full frames can take moderate abuse without falling apart, and the driver doesn't need a pilot's license to understand the controls.

A pickup's versatility makes it a valued member of the family. It can be used to commute to work during the week. On weekends it becomes a workhorse, hauling anything from peat moss to your camper or boat. Install a plow and you can clear your driveway of snow. Order an extended cab and the children can go along for the ride. In fact, these trucks handle family duty better than ever with their standard antilock rear brakes—which prevent the rear wheels from skidding in an emergency—a feature many cars still lack.

It's no wonder pickups have become one of the best-selling vehicle categories in the U.S. Like any piece of valued equipment, they are a major purchasing decision. With that in mind, we've assembled six of the most popular pickup models, both compact and full size, from Ford, Chevrolet and Dodge, in various configurations.

I've used these pickups as you would: not on a race track but in the real world, the world of potholes, bumper-to-bumper traffic, interstates and backroads. I have not only driven these trucks, but worked them at home. The test results will give you a feel for each truck's distinct personality and features to help you decide which one's right for you.

Compact Trucks

Ford Ranger (Regular Cab)

Wheel base: 107.9"
Engine: 100-hp I-4
Observed fuel mileage: 20.5 mpg
Standard payload rating: 1,200 lbs.
Base price: $9,001
Price as tested: $10,464

Our two-wheel drive Ranger was delivered with mid-level XLT interior trim and the regular (6-foot) cargo box, along with the standard 5-speed manual transmission. Other noteworthy options included a split bench seat with armrest, AM/FM stereo cassette player, air conditioning, sliding rear window and all-season tires. The Ranger is available in SuperCab, four-wheel drive (4WD) and long wheelbase versions.

All Ranger models benefit from a redesigned front to give them the look of Ford's big F-Series pickups. Inside, there's a new dash with complete instrumentation, including a tachometer. Of special interest is the newly designed standard 2.3 liter dual-plug engine. This engine, based on a previous design, uses two spark plugs per cylinder for better performance and fuel economy, and also is equipped with fuel injection and a fully electronic ignition system that eliminates the distributor cap.

This engine surprised me with its smoothness and ample power compared to the old design, especially when combined with the smooth-shifting five-speed transmission. Ford introduced a more powerful 4.0-liter V6 for 1990, but the dual-plug engine should be adequate if you carry a light load most of the time. The Ranger's comfortable, contoured bench seat is covered with attractive velour to help prevent you from sliding around. The same material is used on the door panels, creating a very warm and inviting interior.

Controls are very user-friendly, especially the multi-function lever that controls the interval wipers, turn signals, and high beams, and the simple slide-lever climate controls. A coin box and compartments in both doors provide storage space. There's also plenty of head room, with ample shoulder room for two people, but it's a tight squeeze for three.

The Ranger's cargo box is equipped with stake holes, plus support pockets that accept two 2-by-6-inch boards, so standard 4-by-8 sheets of material can fit in the bed with the tailgate down. The tailgate can be easily removed to avoid scratching the inside surface and is light enough for one person to remove and install.

Overall, the Ranger we drove impressed us with its high-quality paint finish and rattle-free construction, good fuel economy and comfortable interior. It's an outstanding value for the money.

Chevrolet S-10 4WD (Regular Cab)/GMC S-15

Wheelbase: 108.3" (short bed)

Engine : 160-hp V6
Observed fuel mileage: 18.4 mpg
Standard payload rating: 1,000 lbs.
Base price: $11,275
Price as tested: $15,260

The S-10 we drove demonstrated the versatility of a pickup truck, combining the performance of a V6 engine and the utility of shift-on-the-fly 4WD. Our well-appointed S-10 with Tahoe interior trim featured a four-speed automatic transmission, regular cargo bed, chrome-step bumper, power windows and door locks, alloy wheels, air conditioning, as well as a tilt steering wheel, AM/FM stereo with cassette and a cloth bench seat. Chevrolet also offers the S-10 in a long-bed and Maxi-Cab versions, with 2WD or 4WD. The S-10 is virtually identical to the GMC S-15 Jimmy pickup truck.

The S-10's optional fuel-injected, 4.3-liter V6 is also the base powerplant for the fullsize C-15 pickup, and essentially is a small block V8 less two cylinders. The engine is smooth and responsive, aided by the column-mounted automatic transmission, and is rated at a hefty 230-pounds-foot of torque at 2,800 rpm. This engine's proven design should be as durable as its legendary big brother. There are two other engines available: a 2.4-liter four-cylinder and a 2.8-liter V-6.

The interior of the S-10 is more carlike than most pickups, as major controls are grouped around the steering wheel within easy reach. I appreciated the handy map lights contained in the rearview mirror, and the tilt steering wheel. Three adults can fit in the bench seat without too much squeezing, but the seat lacks enough support for long stints behind the wheel. Storage areas are in the doors and behind the seat. A shift lever on the floor engages the 4WD.

One editor using the S-10 to haul compost out of soft ground commented favorably on the effective 4WD system, particularly the 4-Lo speed that applies ample torque in extra-slippery situations. The truck tested had the optional 1,500 pound payload package, a worthy option for a mere $64. With this package and larger P235/75R15 on/off-road tires, our S-10 had a notably stiff ride when unloaded, but well within the tolerable range.

The big wheels and tires, slick two-tone paint, high ground clearance, and V6 engine give the S-10 a sporty look and feel. With a wide range of functional and appearance options, compact truck buyers can tailor models to their needs.

Dodge Dakota Sport

Wheelbase: 112" (short bed)
Engine: 125-hp V6
Observed fuel mileage:16 mpg
Standard payload rating:1,250 lbs.

Base price: $14,425 (2WD)
Price as tested: $16,595

Without a doubt, the Dakota attracted the most attention of all the vehicles in our test. The Dakota also is a mid-sized truck, a bit larger than the compact trucks, offering a longer and wider cargo bed.

Our 4WD Dakota Sport had a 3.9-liter V6 engine and an optional four-speed automatic transmission. Standard features on the model include a tachometer, power steering, power windows and door locks, a grippy velour seat with armrest and a comfortable leather-wrapped steering wheel. Outside, there are large P215/75R-15 mud and snow tires on cast aluminum wheels.

Its 6 1/2 foot-bed is a true workhorse. I used the Dakota to haul more than 500 pounds of slate and sand for my patio, a chore I wouldn't want to do with my economy sedan. There are more work-oriented hardtop Dakotas available with short or long wheelbases, and either 2WD or 4WD. The base engine is Chrysler's durable 2.5-liter four-cylinder engine. The fuel-injected V6 engine, another design derived from a V8, provided adequate but not overwhelming power. The Dakota's instrument panel is extremely readable, with clearly marked instruments, and has a handy cup holder.

If you're looking for a pickup for both personal and work purposes, the Dakota is for you.

Full Size Pickups

Ford F-150 (Regular Cab)

Wheelbase: 133.0" (long bed)
Engine: 185-hp V8
Observed fuel mileage: 15.4 mpg
Standard payload rating: 1,735 lbs.
Base price: $10,716
Price as tested: $15,939

A familiar sight at work sites, on the farm and in suburbia, the best-selling Ford F-Series has improved through steady evolution since the current platform was introduced as a 1980 model. The front end was given a more aerodynamic look in 1987, but the truck maintains its traditional styling. More important, Ford updated its powertrains, recently adding multi-port fuel injection on all engines to assure optimum power and fuel economy.

Our test truck was equipped with the optional 5.0-liter V8 and column mounted four speed automatic transmission, in luxurious XLT Lariat trim. The trim package includes such amenities as air conditioning, an auxiliary fuel tank, cruise control, additional insulation and power door locks and windows. Our F-150 had a very comfortable one-piece bench seat with a folding arm rest. A myriad of 4WD, SuperCab, short- and long-bed models are available for the F-150 and F-250, with several engine choices: the base 4.9-liter six-cylinder, and two V8's.

If pickup trucks are friendly, then the F-150 is probably the friendliest of all, since all the controls are instantly familiar. The floorboard-mounted highbeam switch shows this model's age, as does the dash-mounted windshield wiper knob. The instruments are clearly marked, with excellent windshield visibility. The power windows/door locks and cruise controls can be operated by feel, making the interior a nice place to be for long periods. And the old-fashioned vent windows work as well as ever.

Ride control is solid over both smooth and rutted roads, and the power steering and brakes offer the driver good road feel. In fact, once acclimated, the F-150 drives a lot smaller than it looks. The V8 has enough power to pass with ease, and the truck's auxiliary fuel tank gave us an over 400-mile range without a fill-up. When it was time to perform some hauling chores, its long pickup bed easily carried 4-by-8 plywood sheets.

After driving the F-150, I'm not surprised it's one of the most popular vehicles on the road today. It has a roomy, comfortable interior, a proven reliability record, impressive cargo capacity, and costs less than many four-door sedans.

Chevrolet C-1500 (Extended Cab)

Wheelbase: 141.5" (short bed)
Engine: 210-hp V8
Observed fuel mileage: 17.5 mpg
Standard payload rating: 1,908 lbs.
Base price: $11,716
Price as tested: $16,549

Introduced with great fanfare in 1987 as a 1988 model, the completely redesigned fullsize Chevrolet pickup truck has become GM's best selling-vehicle. With a fire-burning V8 engine under the hood, room for three in the back seat and stunning styling, the C-1500 is representative of how flexible as pickup can be with the right choice of options, in this case, turning the truck into both a workhorse and a family sedan. The Chevrolet C/K series is similar to the GMC Sierra pickup.

Many convenience options were included on our test vehicle, including a four-speed automatic transmission, an electric climate control system, and a roomy center console with cupholders between the bucket seats. The most useful feature, however, was the extra room behind the front seats. Although it's a bit difficult to slide past the folding front passenger seat, the rear bench seat features armrests, ample head and leg room, deep storage pockets on either side, and three-point shoulder/lap belts for outboard passengers. If you need more cargo room, the seat folds away.

Thanks to the generous amount of glass in the Chevy's two large doors, as well as the two tall side windows in the extended cab, the truck's interior is bright and cheery. The tweed cloth covering the seats makes for a comfortable ride. The unique disc-type gauges and numerous buttons on the dash took a while to adjust to but contribute to this truck's high-tech look and feel.

If the electronic displays and the slick interior have you feeling a bit confused, open the hood. There you'll find an old friend, Chevy's venerable 5.7-liter V8-updated with fuel injection, electronic controls and a self-adjusting serpentine fan belt. Plenty of room on either side of the engine allows for easy changing of the spark plugs. If the short wheelbase model doesn't fit your needs, there's a long wheelbase version with an extended or regular cab, and either 2WD or 4WD (K1500). The engine choices include a 4.3-liter V6, a 5.0-liter and a 5.7-liter V8.

Overall, this Chevrolet has an extremely supple ride, outstanding engine performance with good economy, and excellent brakes. With its family-sized interior, the C-1500 Extended Cab Pickup blurs the line between cars and trucks in terms of comfort and convenience, while maintaining its considerable utility value.

Dodge Ram D250 (Regular Cab)

Wheelbase: 131" (long bed)
Engine: 160-hp I-6 diesel
Observed fuel mileage: 17.2 mpg
Standard payload rating: 2,893 lbs.
Base price: $11,722
Price as tested: $18,147

The only three-quarter-ton pickup in the group, we chose this model because it's available with the all new Cummins turbocharged diesel engine (a $2,400 option). Designed for hard-work applications, the truck has power steering, high-capacity cooling and electrical systems, an auxiliary oil cooler, underhood service light and extra insulation in the hood, dash and floor. It also has a 30-gallon fuel tank, giving the truck a more than 400-mile range.

Cummins is a well-known supplier of engines to the truck industry. Although new to Dodge, this engine has been in production since 1984, powering a variety of heavy duty vehicles. The biggest advantage it has over a gas engine is the high torque (400 pounds-feet) it develops at a low 1,700 rpm, an excellent combination to have when pulling a large trailer up a steep hill. And since it's turbocharged, the Cummins engine maintains excellent performance in high altitudes.

Our test truck was equipped with the standard Getrag five-speed manual transmission with overdrive; a three speed automatic is also available. When the truck arrived, I immediately opened the hood and was struck by the clean, uncluttered layout of the engine, especially the turbocharger, which is in full view. With plenty of room on either side of the engine, routine maintenance should be easy. You can also select one of three gasoline-powered engines—a 3.9-liter V6, and 5.2- and 5.9-liter V8s—for the D250. A 4WD Power Ram (W250) model is offered as well.

In actual use, there's no doubt the Cummins diesel overpowers the Dodge's personality with the characteristic diesel clatter. The transmission is very positive but notchy in its operation, and I quickly found myself bypassing first gear altogether in regular driving, since its ratio is best suited for towing duty. The overdrive fifth gear minimizes engine noise, while still providing outstanding acceleration with none of the turbo or diesel lag I've come to expect from other turbocharged vehicles.

The rest of the Dodge seems solid enough, with a well-padded bench seat and a molded plastic storage compartment behind it. The dash looks a bit dated compared to the other trucks, but all the controls are within easy reach. With its burly engine, 8-foot bed, jumbo 16-inch tires and chiseled masculine exterior, the D250 may be the ideal work/camper/tow vehicle.

reserved. For a one-year subscription send $18 to <u>Organic Gardening</u>, 33 E. Minor St., Emmaus, PA 18098.

☆ ☆ ☆ ☆ ☆

Chapter Ten

Best American Tires

☆ ☆ ☆ ☆ ☆

Firestone, Uniroyal, Goodyear, Goodrich: Of these once great American tire manufacturers, only one remains independent. We are in the midst of a globalization of the tire industry and only Goodyear has survived the process intact. Several years ago, in an effort to forestall the inevitable, Goodrich and Uniroyal merged. However, in 1989, the French tire maker Michelin bought out Uniroyal-Goodrich. The second-last remaining American tire company, Firestone, was acquired by the Japanese tire company Bridgestone in 1989.

Tires from all of these companies are made in many countries around the world. You can find Dunlop, Bridgestone, Michelin and Pirelli made in the U.S.A. Similarly, you can find Goodyear tires made in France, West Germany and many other countries. All tires have the country of origin marked on the tire itself.

Almost every Goodyear tire sold in the United States is manufactured in the United States. Tires are difficult to shop for because not every tire comes in a size that will fit your car or truck, and only certain tires are recommended for specific vehicles. However, in general, there is a Goodyear tire which is recommended for every car, foreign or domestic.

Goodyear makes many original equipment tires, tires which are made for specific new cars. Goodyear acquired the Kelly-Springfield Tire Company in the early 1980s. Kelly-Springfield makes replacement tires in the United States under many different brand names, which will be listed later in this chapter.

Goodyear Tires

Goodyear tires are widely regarded as among the best in the world. Chrysler, Ford, Honda and Volkswagen recently awarded Goodyear quality awards. That Goodyear is chosen as the original equipment on many prestigious cars is a testament to the quality of their tires. For example, the Ferrari F40, the Corvette ZR-1, the Ford Taurus SHO and the Thunderbird Supercharged Coupe sport Goodyear original equipment tires. Many of Japan's performance cars have Goodyears as original equipment including the Nissan "Z", Mazda RX-7 and Toyota Supra.

High Performance Tires

Without a doubt, Goodyear's **Eagle** line of tires are the world's best high performance tires. In addition to the the sports cars mentioned above many BMWs come equipped with the Goodyear Eagle NCT radial tire, shipped from Union City, Tennessee to West Germany. The most expensive American car, the Cadillac Allante, comes equipped with Goodyear Eagles.

I have driven for many years on Eagles. The only complaint that I have is that traction in rain and snow is limited. Goodyear responded to this complaint in 1986 by rolling out the Eagle GT+4, an all-season performance tire. If you have a sporty sedan, or a high-performance sports car, consider the Eagle GT+4 when replacing your tires.

The Ferrari F40 will go over 200 miles per hour. Because Eagle tires are built to handle the Ferrari's ultra-high speeds, they are very expensive. For those of us who keep normal driving speeds in double-digits we recommend the all-season Vector or Double-Eagle tires.

All Season Radial Tires

In 1988 Goodyear introduced the **Double Eagle** premium passenger car tire. This all-season radial tire carries a 60,000 mile tread warranty, free tire replacement for tread life for defects in workmanship and material, as well as lifetime balancing, alignment checks, rotation and tire inspection. I recommend this tire for luxury cars. The warranty is the best of its kind for any tire made in the world.

The **Vector** all-season radial and the **Invicta** are basically the same tire. Both are premium tires, a notch below the Double Eagle, but excellent tires nonetheless. The Vector earned high snow traction marks in consumer testing by West German auto club members and taxi fleets in the United States.

Off the Road Vehicle Tires

Wrangler tires are recommended for all-terrain vehicles, four-wheel drive applications, pick-up trucks and other vehicles in which traction in mud and snow is essential. The new $600,000 presidential Lincoln limousine was outfitted with a custom-made set of Wrangler tires, just in case there was an emergency need to drive in mud or snow. This tire is used on many Jeep vehicles and has extra-deep tread needed for traction.

Selecting Replacement Tires

When your tread is down to a quarter of an inch or less it is time to replace your tires. Find out what tires are recommended for your car. Unfortunately, you can't test drive tires. If you want to buy the best American tires (which are the best tires in the world), look for the Goodyear label. As mentioned earlier, Goodyear acquired the Kelly-Springfield Tire Company. Kelly makes high-quality replacement tires under its own name and under various other brand names. The following companies sell tires made by Kelly-Springfield:

Vogue
Shell Oil
Unical
Lee-Star
Sears
Summit
Monarch
Montgomery Ward

Vogue Tires are sold exclusively through Cadillac dealerships. They are luxury radial tires and will fit Lincolns, Mercedes and many other large cars. They cost about $150 each.

Shell, Unical, Montgomery Ward and Sears sell hundreds of thousands of Kelly-Springfield tires under their own labels. To find out if a tire is manufactured by Kelly look at the DOT code along the rim of the tire. If the number begins with a "P," the tire is an American-made Kelly-Springfield. Kelly produces millions of tires every year, and its private label tires are a good source of tire "deals." They can be good values because most of these private labels spend very little on advertising.

☆ ☆ ☆ ☆ ☆

Chapter Eleven

Stereo Equipment

☆ ☆ ☆ ☆ ☆

America has long been one of the world's innovators in the design and production of stereo components. Such respected names as McIntosh, Harman Kardon and Acoustic Research originated in the United States. These companies and others produced many of the leading edge components in the fifties and sixties. However, by the seventies the Japanese had either bought, or forced many of these companies from the market. Today, there is a thriving American audio industry concentrating on the mid and higher end components and speakers.

Stereo Rack Systems

Don't buy a stereo rack system. According to Edward Myer, a leading accoustical expert, rack systems "sport a truly amazing array of useless lights, meters, dials, switches and knobs, with lots of raw power and large impressive speakers boxes containing an assortment of low quality tweeters, midranges and woofers. Obviously most of these One Brand Rack Stereos were designed to appeal to the lowest common denominator of taste and musical discernment. Because of their technical inferiority, I would suggest avoidance."

Myer also recommends buying speakers first. Speakers are the most important component of any stereo system because speakers convert electronic impulses into sound waves. Your system is only as good as its speakers.

Speakers

American speakers are the best in the world; while two companies manufacture compact disk players in the U.S., there are literally hundreds of speaker manufacturers. This is one area of technology where the Americans win hands down.

You don't have to spend a fortune to buy a good pair of speakers. Henry Kloss, designer of the original **Acoustic Research** and **Advent** speakers, and founder of KLH, has recently founded **Cambridge SoundWorks**. Kloss says: "It's no trick to design outstanding equipment if cost is no object. The challenge is to achieve high performance at reasonable cost."

Cambridge SoundWorks speakers have received unanimous praise from stereo reviewers. Cambridge produces three different speakers systems: **Ensemble** ($500 pair), **Ambiance** ($220-$260 pair) and **Model Eleven** ($600 system). The Ensemble was Cambridge's first model, and the reviewers found it to be comparable to systems costing twice as much. It includes four speakers, two sub-woofers and two satellite speakers for mid and higher sounds. Ambiance are state-of-the-art bookshelf speakers. The Model Eleven is a portable stereo with an amplifier, but without a CD or tape player, it is a traveling case. These speakers are not available in stores. They must be ordered direct from the factory at (800) AKA-HIFI.

The Ensemble system is pictured above.

The Ambiance speakers are pictured above.

One of the leading speaker manufacturers is the **Carver Corporation** based in Lynnwood, Washington. The company was founded in 1979 by Bob Carver, who also founded the Phase Linear Corporation (now owned by International Jensen, see below).

Carver now holds several patents on new stereo technology including their Sonic Holography, which has been licensed to Toshiba for use in some of their televisions; sonic holography technology can help make recorded music sound almost live.

Another high-quality speaker system, **Magnepan** "Maggies" don't look like ordinary speakers—they look more like room dividers because they are only two inches thick. Maggies are ribbon speakers, also known as dipole radiators, invented by James Winey, an engineer with 3M company, who developed the concept in 1966. Since the Magnepans hit the market in 1972 more than 100,000 pairs have been sold around the world. The smallest Maggies are 4 feet high ($575 a pair), the largest 6 feet high ($2200 a pair). The only complaint I heard was from Howard Blumenthal of the *New York Times* who noted that Maggies are ideal for jazz and classical music, but may not have enough bass for serious rock n' rollers. Blumenthal still found Magnepans to be his speakers of choice.

Magnepan speakers are shown above.

Inside Track an industry newsletter ranked different audio/video manufacturers based on dealer responses. According to dealers, **Polk Audio** was the best manufacturer in both home and car audio speakers in 1988. In addition, *AudioVideo International* magazine had Polk ranked as the number one speaker company from 1983-86 in their yearly top 20 poll. Pretty heady stuff for a company that was founded in 1972 by a group of college buddies from Johns Hopkins University.

International Jensen is another well-respected American manufacturer of stereo speakers. The company markets its products under the **Jensen, Phase Linear** and **Advent** labels. The flagship label, Jensen, was founded 60 years ago and has been an innovator ever since. Jensen was the first company to design and manufacture a car loudspeaker and the first to use graphite materials in their speakers. Advent speakers were introduced in the sixties on the premise of providing high quality two-way design speakers to consumers. The Advent label is known for its well respected line of home speakers which include the **Prodigy** and **Baby Advent** models. Both of these models were quite favorably reviewed by leading audiophile and consumer magazines. The company's third label produces high quality loudspeakers for cars, trucks and vans under the **Phase Linear** label.

Infinity has also been a highly regarded American producer of quality loudspeakers. The company's flagship speakers are the IRS (Industry Reference Standard) V speakers which retail for an incredible $50,000! Infinity realizes that the average consumer can not afford these speakers, but the company believes that the advances from engineering speakers of this quality filter down to its other products. Infinity speakers start at about $200 a pair for excellent quality bookshelf speakers, its model 1001.

Bose Corporation of Framingham, Massachusetts, manufactures a range of top-quality speakers. Bose developed the direct/reflective or omnidirectional type of loudspeaker which fills a room with sound. Bose's entry-level 201 speakers cost about $200 a pair. The top-of-the-line Bose 901s are about $1,200 a pair.

Dahlquist sounds Swedish, but is all-American. Dahlquist speakers are topnotch, ranging in price from $500 a pair for bookshelf speakers to a $2000 a pair floor model.

The plethora of American speaker manufacturers is so great that it becomes nearly impossible to review every American speaker in all price ranges. In addition to the brands we mention above, the following list represents what we consider to be ten of the best American manufacturers of loudspeakers covering a range of styles and prices (in alphabetical order):

1. **Acoustic Research**
2. **Bose**
3. **Boston Acoustic**
4. **Cambridge SoundWorks**
5. **Cerwin-Vega**
6. **Dahlquist**
7. **Infinity**
8. **Jensen (including Advent and Phase Linear)**
9 **Magnepan**
10. **Polk**

There are many small speaker companies that produce excellent products. One of those, **NHT (Now Hear This)**, of Benicia, California makes the most dramatic looking, and good-sounding, speakers, in both bookshelf and floor models. To find a retail store near you call NHT's toll-free number: (800) 648-9993. Another California company, **Wilson Audio** of Nevato, makes world-class speakers ranging in price from $6,000 to $85,000 a pair. **SPICA** of Albuquerque, NM makes high-quality speakers from $400 to $1,300 a pair.

Good speakers are in the ears of the beholder. You must listen to speakers for yourself, and decide which speakers sound best to you.

Amplifiers and Pre-Amps

Carver manufactures some, but not all of its products, in the United States. Those products produced in the United States include their four top-of-the-line amplifiers which retail for between $800 and $1,000. Three of five preamplifiers manufactured by Carver are produced domestically; those models made in the USA are the C-11, the C-16 and the C-19. Prices for these components range from $580 to $1200.

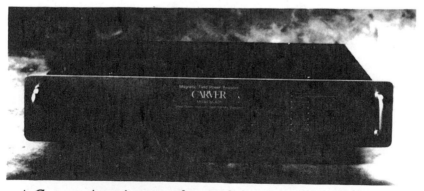

A Carver American-made amplifier is pictured above.

Another domestic stereo component manufacturer is **Counterpoint Electronic Systems** which designs and produces all of its products in the United States. Counterpoint's products are among the highest quality sold on the market and are among the most expensive. Its entry level preamplifier retails for just under $1,000. The most expensive piece in the Counterpoint product line is the SA-9/11 preamplifier system that retails for $10,000 (the world's most expensive!). Counterpoint systems employ a hybrid of solid state and the more old fashioned vacuum tube technology to achieve what they consider the finest built equipment on the market today.

The grandfather of all American stereo makers is still in business today. **McIntosh Laboratory** first began to manufacture products in 1949. The company still maintains a strong commitment to the industry by producing hardware dedicated to the serious music lover. Many McIntosh components contain sophisticated signal processing devices that are invaluable to anyone with a large collection of old irreplaceable records whose sound quality may have diminshed some over the years.

A McIntosh amplifier is pictured above.

Sumo (yes, it's American) of Chatsworth, California, makes top-rated amplifiers and pre-amps. Sumo's 60 watt amplifier sells for about $500.

Audio Research Corporation (Minneapolis, MN) makes fine top-end amps and pre-amps. Its LS1 preamp is world class in performance and price ($1500). Audio Research's Classic 60 Hybrid tube designed amplifier retails for over $3,000.

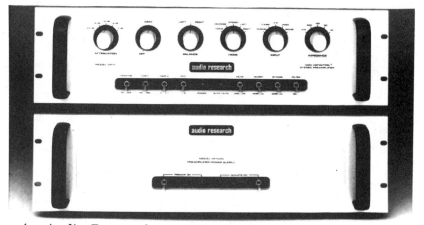

An Audio Research amplifier is shown above.

Compact Disk Players

There are two high-quality manufacturers of compact disk players in the United States, **California Audio Labs** and **McIntosh Laboratories**. Cal Audio makes two models, **Icon** and **Tercet**. Icon ($700) was top-rated in a recent audio magazine, and the Tercet performs a notch better for twice the price.

The California Labs Icon is pictured above.

McIntosh, known for its amplifiers, makes a world-class compact disk player. Its suggested retail price is $2,000.

The McIntosh MCD7007 is shown above.

Turntables

We have found only one American manufacturer of stereo turntables. Most people use their old turntables or use CD players or tape decks. Some stereo buffs prefer to play records. **SOTA (State of the Art)** of Berkeley, CA, makes turntables for audiophiles ranging in price from $895 to $4,500.

☆ ☆ ☆ ☆ ☆

Chapter Twelve

Televisions and Video Cassette Recorders

☆ ☆ ☆ ☆ ☆

If one were to chart the number of American-owned and foreign-owned manufacturers of televisions over the last twenty years, the resulting graphs would be mirror images of each other. In 1968, there were eighteen U.S.-owned manufacturers of televisions; by 1989 that number had dropped to just one—**Zenith.** The first foreign-owned producer of televisions did not arrive until 1972, but by 1988 there were a total of seventeen foreign producers in the USA. The situation in video cassette recorders (VCR) is even more startling: even though the VCR was invented in the United States, no American-owned manufacturers of them exist today. There is no VCR wholly manufactured in the USA.

There is a new America entry into the television market—**JBL,** the renowned stereo manufacturer. JBL produces a television system, which projects televised (and taped) images on to flat or curved screens from six to eight feet in size. Prices start at about $4,000. To locate a dealer in your area contact JBL at (818) 895-3498.

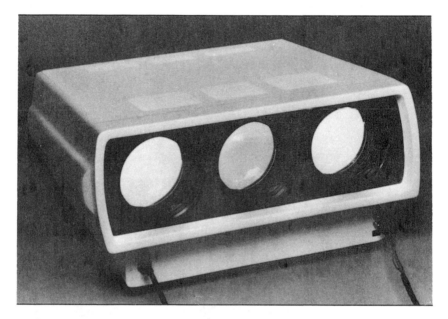

JBL television projector is shown above.

Many companies produce large screen televisions in the USA. The decision by these foreign companies to produce televisions in the US, instead of importing them from abroad, is a purely economic one. To produce a large screen television—say 19 inch or 20 inch—abroad and then import it to the USA is economically irrational. The cost of shipping bulky whole televisions, or even just picture tubes is prohibitive. In addition, the cost of wood, used in the manufacturing of television cabinets, is much more expensive in the Far East than in the USA. Thus, economically producing large televisions here is much more feasible for foreign companies than importing them from abroad.

Foreign-owned television companies with assembly lines in the United States generally import many of the electronic components that are the brains behind today's televisions. Keep in mind that when many of these companies mention that their televisions have a domestic content of 40, 50 or even 60 percent this number comes almost entirely from the cost of producing just the picture tube and cabinet.

Zenith Televisions

Zenith Electronics is the only surviving American manufacturer of televisions in the USA. The company operates several factories in Illinois and a plant in Tijuana, Mexico. Zenith makes televisions ranging from 9-inch to 45-inch projection models. Zenith assembles its smallest models (9-inch and 13-inch) in Mexico and makes some components for its larger televisions there as well. All other Zenith televisions, ranging from 19-inch tabletop models to their projection television systems, are manufactured in the United States. Zenith manufactures a competitively priced and highly reliabe line of televisions. Many of Zenith's larger models contain some of the most advanced features and sound available on the market today. However, Zenith does not manufacture its own video cassette recorders (VCR). VCRs with a Zenith label are made abroad by JVC for the company.

Zenith's 1991 line of televisions feature many superior models. Several of these televisions feature Bose sound systems which produce hifi quality sound to accompany the picture. Other Zenith 1990 models offer premium stereo which offer excellent sound and the capability to add surround sound.

The most impressive feature in the new Zenith line is digital television, which has a number of advantages over analog televisions. Digital TV offers "picture in a picture viewing," meaning that while watching one program you can view another channel's picture simultaneously in one corner of the screen. Digital technology also allows for switching the large picture with the insert and freezing the insert picture. This technology is so sophisticated that up to four different channels can be displayed on the screen simultaneously.

A Zenith 46-inch rear projection set is pictured above.

Video Cassette Recorders

Although invented in the United States by Ampex Corporation in 1954, the video tape recorder was never mass produced by an American company for home use.

Panasonic manufactures a few of its VCRs in the USA. Three models are made at its plant in Vancouver, Washington. The models are the PV 2900 and the PV 4900. The 2900 is a two-head VCR and the 4900 is a four-head machine. Also assembled in the USA is the 4920, which includes a bar-code reader for easier programming. The U.S. content on these machines may be less than 50 percent, but it is undeniably higher than similar models produced overseas.

☆ ☆ ☆ ☆ ☆

Chapter Thirteen

Telephones, Cellular Phones and Fax Machines

☆ ☆ ☆ ☆ ☆

The two most recognized names in telephones in the United States are AT&T and Bell. Yet contrary to what most people believe, neither company manufactures single-line phones in this country anymore. AT&T continues to manufacture some of its multi-line business telephones in the United States. The only other US manufacturers left in the phone industry are **Comdial** and **ITT/Cortel co**, which is a subsidiary of **Alcatel**, a French company. BellSouth is the only former AT&T subsidiary which markets made in the USA telephones to the consumer, and its phones are manufactured by Cortelco.

The good news is that in cellular phone technology the United States leads the world. The American presence may be limited to one company, **Motorola**, but it is the dominant player, controlling one quarter of the world market.

Although Americans invented the fax machine the market is dominated by foreign companies; however, fax boards and **Star Signal's** new color fax are two notable exceptions.

Home Telephones

Alcatel and Comdial manufacture an extensive line of personal phones in addition to those marketed for business. Their line of consumer products range from the standard wall and desk phones to more advanced models. BellSouth distributes these phones under their label.

The standard wall and desk phones are still made in the USA.

ITT/Cortelco also markets other phones with more substantial features. An example of this is the **Trendline** phones which include with the standard features three-number emergency autodial, nine number memory and a call directory. The Trendline series of phones are available in nine different designer colors ($44.95).

Alcatel also manufactures the **Citation** and **Tribute** phone series ($44.95- $54.95). Both of these models come with easier to use large indented buttons and a lightweight handset that is comfortable to hold. ITT-Cortelco also markets more advanced models of the Citation and Tribute with conveniences such as last number redial, memory and a pull-out directory for other frequently dialed numbers.

Cellular Telephones

The cellular telephone industry, despite its significant impact on American society, was only introduced in 1983. There are more than 2 million cellular telephones operating in the United States; cellular phone industry experts predict that within five years there will be more than 10 million users in the U.S. Cellular service is currently available to more than 75 percent of the USA.

Despite the enormous growth potential in cellular phones, there is only one company—**Motorola**—making cellular telephones in the United States. Motorola, however, now makes telephones for Sears and Montgomery Ward starting at $200, for **Cincinnati Microwave** and under the **Pulsar** name, Motorola's own low-price label. A leader in developing cellular telephones Motorola has meant quality electronics for over

50 years. The company presently controls about one quarter of the world market. Motorola has assembled one of the most versatile cellular product lines of any manufacturer.

The newly introduced **Micro TAC** Personal Telephone is the smallest and lightest (12.3 ounces) cellular phone for sale. Though the Micro T.A.C. fits in the palm of the hand, it has many of the same functions as larger models; these include 120 number auto memory, auto answer, menu mode and speed dialing. The phone can be recharged in as little as eight hours with Motorola's Intellicharge Rapid Charger. This technological wonder sold for $2500 last year and can now be purchased for under $1,000. The MicroTAC is two years ahead of anything offered by any other cellular manufacturer.

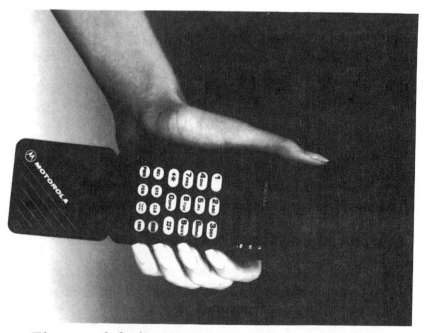

The top-of-the-line MicroTAC is shown above.

The **Tough Talk Transportable,** also made by Motorola, fills another niche in the cellular market. Contained in a rugged, streamlined case weighing under ten pounds, this phone offers at least two full hours of fully transportable use before recharging is necessary. The company also manufactures several cellular phones exclusively for automobiles. These phones can be equipped with the advanced D.V.S.P. II Digital Vehicular Speaker Phone. This fully hands-free option is controlled by a digital microprocessor. The speaker is completely duplex in operation, which allows both parties to speak simultaneously without either being aware that a speaker phone is being employed.

All these models have at least 100 number memory. Other more advanced models offer space diversity reception, which has two antennas working in conjunction to compensate for signal reduction, allowing for clear, continuous reception. Motorola also offers two- system registration to increase a customer's ability to take advantage of their cellular phone. This option enables a consumer to register in two markets or to register both systems in his or her home market.

Three cellular phones are sold under the Pulsar label, the mobile phone, the portable phone and a car telephone. Sears sells these phones under its **America Series** brand. Sears sells the mobile phone, which plugs into your car's cigarette lighter jack for $200. This low price does not include the battery pack, which is not needed for car use. Sears sells the car phone for $400 installed. Montgomery Ward sells these phones under its **Ambassador II** label.

Cincinnati Microwave sells the portable phone for $900 by telephone only ((800) 247-4300). This is the company known for its car radar detectors.

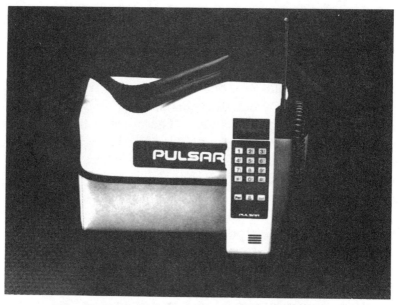

The Pulsar mobile phone is shown above.

The Pulsar car phone is pictured above.

The Pulsar portable phone, sold by Cincinnati Microwave is shown above.

Facsimile Machines

The market for facsimile machines, commonly referred to as "faxes," is nearly completely dominated by the Japanese, with few exceptions. The fax is another technology invented by an American company, AT&T, who failed to capitalize on its invention. AT&T developed a high-quality facsimile machine in the 1920s which was used to transmit wire service photographs. American manufacturers were caught off guard when the desktop fax machine became commonplace in the 1980s. AT&T desktop fax machines are made overseas by Ricoh.

American influence in the industry can be discovered by peering inside a fax machine, in fax boards and in the world's only color fax. Even though there is not a single American manufacturer of stand-alone fax machines, **Rockwell International** supplies over 60 percent of the computer modem circuits found in fax machines. Rockwell's R96F is the world's most popular modem board for use in facsimile machines, with over five million units sold. This small piece of equipment is the "brains" of a fax machine, allowing a machine to send and receive digital signals across phone lines. The rest of a fax machine is basically a telephone and printer packaged together. The quality of Rockwell's product is so high that the boards are shipped directly to factory floors in Japan without going through a quality control check.

There are several American firms that produce circuit boards that, when installed in your personal computer, allow the computer to send and receive messages. The first firm to market this technology was **Brooktrout Technology** in Massachusetts. The company now does about $4 million a year in sales based mainly on their fax board. Nearly all the large mail order computer supply companies sell a fax board for personal computers. Fax circuit boards are less expensive than stand-alone fax machines, and have several other advantages. One advantage is that a computer-driven fax board can send a series of transmissions to many different recipients automatically, with no need for a person to feed documents into it. Another advantage is that incoming and outgoing documents can be stored in computer memory. The last advantage is that documents can be printed on plain paper, by any printer connected to the computer. So, before buying a fax machine, consider buying an American-made fax board.

One up and coming product on the facsimile market also happens to be the only U.S. manufactured fax machine available. **Star Signal Inc.** of Campbell,

California produces the world's first color facsimile machine. The color fax can also function as a color copier or a color scanning and printing peripheral for a computer. The resolution of the **Colorfax** is six times that of a conventional black and white fax machine.

The color fax machine was made commercially viable by Star Signal's ability to reduce the time necessary to scan a document by 50 to 100 times. This means that a one page color document, that once took three hours to scan, can be sent in as little as three minutes. The machine is fully compatible with other Group III monochrome facsimile machines. The main drawback to this technological wonder is its price of $25,900. Information about purchasing a color fax can be obtained from Star Signal at (408) 866-7100.

☆ ☆ ☆ ☆ ☆

Chapter Fourteen

The Home Office

☆ ☆ ☆ ☆ ☆

The American computer industry is fighting back, led by the giant IBM corporation. IBM has just introduced the first American-made laser printer, a multi-billion dollar market, and the moderately priced **PS-1**.

IBM may not be the great innovator that some of the smaller companies are, but it is the industry standard world-wide. In Europe, IBM is the number one computer company.

Best news for the home computer users is the new PS-1 computer, which is priced at $999 for the basic model. It is the most user friendly IBM computer ever introduced. It is also a powerful machine which would have cost three times as much just a few years ago. It is powered to an Intel 80286 microprocessor, with 512 kilobytes of system memory. The PS-1 comes with one 3.5 inch floppy drive, but another floppy or hard-disk

The IBM PS-1 is shown above.

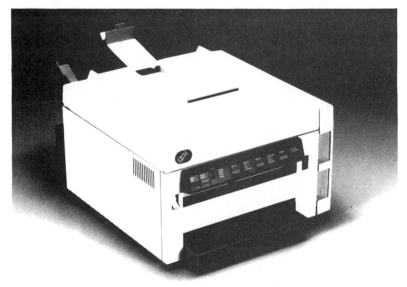

The IBM LaserPrinter is pictured above.

drive is available.

The IBM **LaserPrinter** sells for $1,500, about the same price as Hewlett-Packard's Laserjet. According to *PC Magazine* IBM's printer is better. The magazine awarded the LaserPrinter its Editor's Choice and Technical Excellence awards. IBM's laser printer is made in America, the HP is not.

America is where the personal computer was developed during the seventies. In a California garage, Steve Jobs and Steven Wozniak created the first Apple computer, which launched the personal computer revolution. Even though America is the country that launched the personal computer revolution, it is difficult to assemble a computer today that is completely made in the USA.

From the company's origins in Steven Job's garage, **Apple** has grown into one of America largest companies. The original Apple has grown into a varied product line designed to fit any personal or small business computing needs. Presently, Apple's flagship computer is the Macintosh, which now comes in six different configurations. The basic model is the Macintosh Plus, which is an excellent first computer for a student or a family. As with all the Macintoshes the Plus features easy-to-use, graphics-oriented interface, which is the hallmark of Apple computers.

The next step up in the Macintosh line is the SE and the SE/30 which, unlike the Macintosh Plus, are manufactured in the USA. The main difference between the SE and the SE/30 is that the SE/30 features the newer Intel 68030 microprocessor, which forms the heart of the computer. This newer chip allows the SE/30 to read and write in four different computer operating systems, meaning the SE/30 is compatible with just about any of the other major computers. The Macintosh SE and SE/30 offers many advantages over their predecessor, the Macintosh Plus. The computer comes with more memory, is 20 percent faster and is available with a second disk or internal hard drive. The Macintosh SE and SE/30 also offer a number of expansion slots, which make the computer much more flexible than the Macintosh Plus.

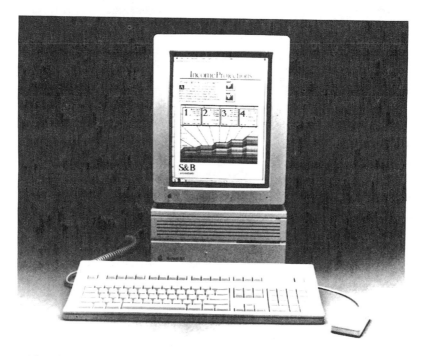

The Macintosh II cx is shown above.

Apple also manufactures its top of the line Macintosh IIs in the United States. The Macintosh II computers offer more versatility than the standard Macintoshes. These newer Macintoshes allow the owner to easily upgrade the computer, and to add-on components in a way that was not possible with earlier models of the computer. Apple also offers the IIx and IIcx, in addition to the standard Macintosh II. The IIx and IIcx offer the advanced Intel 68030 chip, and a larger memory expansion capability.

Apple manufactures its computer components both here and in the Far East. For example, Apple manufactures its Imagewriter II and Imagewriter LQ printer in the Far East, but produces the Imagewriter here in the USA. Apple manufactures its hard disk drives, mouse and fax/modem (this is different than their plain modem which is made in Hong Kong) here in the USA. Other Apple computers and products are not manufactured in the USA.

A relative newcomer to the computer scene, **Datacomp,** is manufacturing IBM-compatible computers in the USA and it is doing so in a union shop. Its prices are competitive and its products are as American as you can get. To find a Datacomp dealer near you call (703) 848-0788.

Another American computer manufacturer is the **Tandy Corporation,** the parent company for **Radio Shack.** Tandy also recently signed an agreement with Panasonic to manufacture computers to be sold under the Panasonic label, for sale in the U.S. and Japan. A company spokesperson at Tandy said this was the first time that an American company had exported computers to Japan.

Tandy manufactures all of the 1000 line of computers in the USA. These computers range from the less expensive Tandy 1000 HX to the more sophisticated 1000 TL model. The basic 1000 HX is a computer designed for computer neophytes; unlike most personal computers the 1000 HX features "instant on."

This allows a user to turn on the computer and move right in to the application without any intermediate steps. The 1000 line of Tandy computers also offers the DeskMate graphics-oriented interface; this feature makes the Tandy computers among the most user-friendly on the market. The other models in the 1000 line offer advanced features. The 1000 TL includes a built-in 80,000 word spell checker and the ability to record and playback sound. The 1000 SL also has more memory, three disk drive capability and either a 3.5 inch or 5.25 inch disk drive option.

Tandy also manufactures the more sophisticated, and faster, 3000 NL. It is fully IBM-compatible, and is available with a fixed-disk drive.

Commodore is another American manufacturer of reasonably priced quality computer equipment. The company manufactures the entry level 64C and 128D home computers. The 128D has memory expandable to 640K from 128. This computer also features a numeric keyboard, 16 colors and advanced sound capabilities. The Commodore 64C and 128D are supported by over 10,000 different software programs.

The company also manufactures the Amiga 500 and Amiga 2000 for users who seek a more powerful computer. The Amiga 500 is equipped with 512K of memory which is expandable to one megabyte and has a built-in 3.5 inch disk drive. The more advanced Amiga 2000 comes standard with one megabyte of memory that can be enlarged to an incredible nine megabytes. One of the best features of the Amiga 2000 is its excellent color graphics and sound capabilities. These features give the Amiga 2000 the ability to perform desktop publishing, computer aided design and desktop video functions. Dollar for dollar the Amiga is one of the most advanced computer systems available on the market today.

Laptops

Even though laptop computers accounted for only $1.75 billion in revenue in 1988, industry experts predict that this part of the market will become increasingly more important. The laptop segment is the fastest growing part of the personal computer market. The largest producer of laptops in the world is Zenith, with about 27 percent of market share. GRiD which controls 11.9 percent of the market is the next largest American concern, although the company is third overall in the world.

GRiD Computers is one of the leading laptop manufacturers in the world. Throughout its history the company has been a leader in the laptop field. In 1982 GRiD introduced the first true laptop computer which weighed ten pounds and could fit in a briefcase. The newest GRiD laptops follow in the tradition of their earlier products. The national computer magazine, *PC Week* rated the GRiD model 1530 as a notch above other laptops. Under the sleek black magnesium case of the 1530 is a sophisticated high performance computer. The specs for the 1530 are comparable to many desktop personal computers.

A Grid laptop is shown above.

The third largest American laptop manufacturer is Tandy Corporation (9.4 percent market share), which is also the parent company of GRiD. In fact, the combined market share for Tandy and its subsidiary GRiD would make the second largest company behind Zenith with 21.3 percent of the world market. A newcomer to the portable market, which could be a powerful competitor, is Apple Computer. Apple introduced the long awaited Macintosh portable in the fall of 1989.

In addition to being the largest laptop manufacturer, **Zenith Data Systems**, has long been regarded as one of the most innovative. The company recently introduced the MinisPort ($1,999) the smallest and lightest computer in their product line. The whole computer is the size of a three ring binder and only an inch thick. The total weight, including the rechargable, replaceable battery pack, is just under six pounds.

In order to achieve such small size and weight

Zenith incorporated several special features in the MinisPort. The most significant change is the introduction of a two inch floppy disk drive. Even though some may question the introduction of a third size of computer disks, Zenith's two inch model has some notable advantages. The two inch disks can hold the same 720K worth of data as a 3.5 inch disk, but the disk drive in the MinisPort uses only 40 percent as much power as the standard 3.5 inch portable computer disk drive.

Zenith also stresses that the two inch format was introduced mainly as a back-up device, not meant to directly challenge the other formats. The MinisPort is equipped with a power-saving, semi-backlit screen that draws on external light whenever possible. The computer also employs a silicon drive that acts as permanent storage which runs faster than a conventional hard drive, though with less memory capacity. The computer is also equipped with a backup battery that will prevent the files on the silicon drive from being erased for about three days after the main battery is exhausted.

Apple recently unveiled its first entry into the laptop market, a portable version of their flagship Macintosh computer. The Macintosh portable will be bulky, 17 pounds, for portables, but will include all the features found on a regular Macintosh. These include a high resolution screen and a mouse. To accommodate the mouse in the confines of a portable Apple is using a track ball instead of a standard mouse. The new Macintosh portable is expected to retail for between $5,800 and $6,500 depending on the configuration purchased. For half the price of the Apple you can buy an **Outbound** Apple-compatible portable computer.

Outbound is smaller and lighter than the portable Mac. To find an Outbound dealer near you call (800) 444-4607.

Word Processors

Smith Corona manufactures a complete line of typewriters and word processors in the United States. Every office needs a typewriter for light typing needs, envelopes, rolodex cards and so forth. Our office has a Smith Corona for these needs. Smith Corona typewriters are available at department and discount stores nearly everywhere. You can buy their basic electronic typewriter, the **XL 1700** for about $150. The **XL 2700** is a similar machine with a 50,000 word spelling checker built-in, the **XD 4700** includes editable memory. The **XD 5700** and the **XD 7700** offer more features.

Smith Corona has gone high-tech on us. Its **Personal Word Processor** is much more than a typewriter. The PWP 1000 ($500) comes with a memory of 32,000 characters and an eight-line liquid crystal display. This word processor also includes a 50,000 word dictionary which automatically checks spelling. If you want a computer only to use as a word processor then a Smith Corona PWP may be just what the doctor ordered.

The Smith Corona PWP is shown above.

The Smith Corona PWP 220 system is pictured above.

A step up from the PWP 1000 is the PWP 3100 ($800). It features a 16-line liquid crystal display. For the same price, Smith Corona offer's a computer-like PWP 5100 which has a 24-line, nine inch television monitor. It is larger than the 3100, and if transportability is a necessity, you would probably prefer the smaller model.

The top-of-the-line Smith Corona word processor is the PWP 220. It features a 12-inch monitor and a built-in disk drive. A 50,000 word dictionary is built-in. The PWP 220 can be matched up with two different printers. The complete system retails for about $1,000.

Photocopy Machines

Xerox invented the dry, instant, copier machine. Xerox still makes the best machines in the business, but has concentrated on large business machines, and left the smal copier field to the imports. The smallest Xerox copier is made overseas. Its least expensive USA-made 5008 model costs around $2,000.

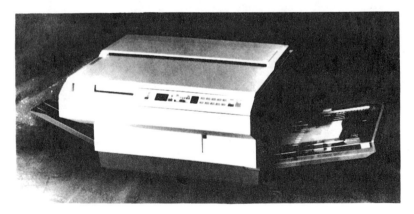

A Xerox 5008 copier is shown above.

☆ ☆ ☆ ☆ ☆

Chapter Fifteen

Home Appliances

☆ ☆ ☆ ☆ ☆

We will focus on seven small appliances in this chapter: toasters, blenders, food processors, coffee makers, microwave ovens, fans and vacuum cleaners. The products we feature are all made domestically, and they all reflect the American spirit of innovation.

We are not reviewing large home appliances like refrigerators, stoves, dishwashers, clothes washers and dryers because nearly all of these are made in the United States. Space does not permit us to include all home appliances.

We are primarily focusing on electrical appliances. However, we would like to explain why we chose not to discuss electric can-openers. There are dozens of imported electric openers on the market, but we still prefer the all-American **Swing-A-Way** manual opener. The Swing-A-Way opener has been manufactured in St. Louis for more than fifty years. Quite frankly, it opens cans more easily than any electric can opener.

Toasters

Proctor-Silex is the world's largest manufacturer of toasters, offering a complete line of toasters and toaster ovens. Their new LOT-A-SLOT Coolwall Toaster ($46.95) features a safe cool-to-the-touch exterior and an easy cleaning crumb tray. The toaster's interior bread slots will also position all bread widths, making it easy to have perfectly toasted breads, bagels, or muffins. Stylistically, the LOT-A-SLOT is quite distinctive. It's sleek, elongated design also serves to save counter space.

Proctor-Silex LOT-A-SLOT is pictured above.

Two other domestic manufacturers offer cool-touch toasters. They are **Black and Decker** and **Toastmaster**. Black and Decker's safe-to-touch toasters offer wide slots for thicker breads and even muffins. The Fastoast model ($37.98) promises to brown your toast twice as fast as conventional toasters, while the Deluxe Fastoast ($44.98) has a keep-warm control to keep your bread warm until it is ready. Black and Decker also makes traditional chrome exterior toasters and toaster ovens.

Toastmaster's cool-touch toasters are priced from $40 to $55.95. These toasters offer many of the convenient features of the others, including wide slots to accommodate pastries. Keep-warm controls and faster toasting features are available on the higher priced cool-touch models. All of Toastmaster's extensive line of toasters and toaster ovens are made in the USA, except Model 775, the pastry toaster.

Sunbeam makes about 80 percent of their appliances in America, and their line of two- and four-slice toasters includes one of the most interesting toasters on the market. The Model 20030 is believed to be the oldest toaster in continuous production. First introduced in 1945, sales are still going strong despite the $84.95 suggested retail price. Today, it retains the timeless Art Deco exterior, yet the toaster is one of the most sophisticated on the market. It is a fully automatic, self-lowering toaster with a unique Radiant Control feature that "senses" the amount of moisture in the bread, allowing for a more uniform toast.

Blenders

Sunbeam prides itself on innovation, and their innovative spirit is reflected in the Model 04101 blender

($34.95); it handles a full four-cup capacity, yet the jar can be inverted to be stored in half the space. Sunbeam also makes a food processor that can accommodate an attachment which transforms the unit into a blender. Look for it in the next section on food processors.

Black and Decker offers two compact blenders. Of special interest is a cordless Handyblender that is powerful enough to chop ice ($51.98). A Handy Slenderbender is also available. It is a cordless portable hand blender designed to be used directly in glasses. With two variable speeds, this blender is perfect for making drinks.

Oster makes a complete line of home appliances, but of the appliances we feature, only their blenders and Kitchen Centers are manufactured domestically. Components of Oster blenders are made in the USA and most of them are assembled in this country, but some are also assembled in Mexico. Don't be shy about turning the product over to check the country of origin if you decide to purchase an Oster blender.

Food Processors

Oster's Kitchen Center products are made in the USA and they include some of the most innovative and convenient appliances on the market. The touch control "5-in-1" Kitchen Center ($300) combines five appliances; it is a blender, stand mixer, doughmaker, slicer/shredder and food processor all in one. The Kitchen Center consists of one central unit with 16 speed settings and different attachments to perform an endless variety of tasks. The set also includes two large mixing bowls and a 250-recipe cookbook. Other attachments can be purchased separately, including a juicer and an ice cream maker.

Oster's Kitchen Center is shown above.

Regal, based in Kewaskum, Wisconsin, makes a versatile food processor that proudly displays a made in the USA emblem on the packaging. The K663BK food processor ($117) is capable of the same functions as more expensive processors, everything from beating eggs to kneading dough. It features a direct drive motor, eliminating problems with stretched belts and eventual belt breakage. There is also a safety function in the cover—the machine will not operate until the cover is securely locked in place. All of the removable parts are easy to clean in a sink or dishwasher.

For smaller food processing needs, Black and Decker's Model HC8 mincer/chopper ($29.98) makes the frequent chopping of onions, garlic and even nuts easier than ever. A Super Chopper is also available for $37.98; it has double the capacity of most small mincer/choppers, and it comes with a whipping attachment.

Coffeemakers

One out of every two Americans drink coffee, and sales of gourmet beans have soared in recent years, reflecting a growing sophistication in the American coffee drinker. American coffeemaker manufacturers have kept pace with the demanding public.

Black and Decker is one of the leading designers in coffeemakers. They offer several models that brew coffee directly into a thermal carafe. The unique carafe can keep coffee warm for up to eight hours. The outer body is made of molded plastic, making the carafe an attractive beverage server as well. The Thermal Carafe Coffee Maker retails for $58, and a model with 24-hour analog timer sells for $75. The company's Spacemaker Plus line also has two thermal-carafe coffeemakers. They install under cabinets to maximize counterspace without sacrificing full capacity. The PDC403A has a digital timer, and retails for $112. The distinctive Spacemaker Plus was justifiably honored with the Industrial Design Excellence Award in 1988. Under-the-cabinet coffeemakers with glass carafes are available in the company's Spacemaker line.

Black and Decker's counter-top coffeemakers are no less stunning in design, as exemplified by the Model DCM328F ($55). The stark 10-cup coffeemaker has a permanent gold filter to improve coffee taste.

Proctor-Silex coffeemakers come with a patented Hydro-Clean system to fight water mineral build up, thus maintaining brewing speed and extending the life of the appliance. The contemporary styled A6306 coffeemaker features a 24-hour digital timer and a convenient pause/serve function that allows you to fill your first cup of coffee without interrupting the brewing process. This coffee maker has a 12-cup capacity, and retails for $39.99.

The Proctor-Silex A6306 is shown above.

Regal also offers a 12-cup automatic drip coffee maker with 24-hour timer. The K7586 is white colored, available with either mocha brown or slate blue accents ($50.00).

Mr. Coffee is a famous American name in coffee-makers, but unfortunately many of their products are imported. In the future, however, new owners are aiming to increase domestic production to 50 percent. Again, please check underneath Mr. Coffee's appliances for the country of origin.

Microwave Ovens

The microwave oven is an invention that has changed cooking habits in kitchens across the country. The food industry, appliances and accessories have also been affected by the quick heating oven.

It may be surprising to find out that the microwave was invented in the United States by Raytheon Corporation, and refined by its Amana division. Since the invention of the microwave oven, most of the manufacturing of the product has moved overseas. Now a majority of the microwaves sold in the United States are imported.

Such All-American companies as Litton, General Electric and Sears Amana import their microwave ovens.

Two manufacturers, White Consolidated Industries and Amana, still make microwaves in the United States. WCI produces microwave ovens for Frigidaire, Tappan, Gibson and White-Westinghouse. White Consolidated also exports its microwaves to Europe, South America and the Far East.

Consumer Reports gave the Tappan mid-sized microwave good marks. The Tappan oven is less expensive than most of the comparable imported microwave ovens.

Vacuum Cleaners

Today's American vacuum cleaners have come a long way from the traditional units that only cleaned carpets. Most machines include attachments for cleaning drapes and furniture.

Electrolux, of Marietta, Georgia, has a reputation for making the highest quality vacuum cleaners in the world. Electrolux machines start at about $300 for an upright model, but are designed to last for 20 years.

Oreck has been making commercial vacuum cleaners for 25 years, which are used in many hotels. Oreck has introduced the Oreck XL ($300) for home use. Like Electrolux models this one is built to last.

Bissell produces the **Carpet Machine** which is a wet-dry vacuum which shampoos carpets and rugs with a hot water system. It sells for about $150.

The Hoover Company of North Canton, Ohio, offers one of the most complete lines of cleaners. Some of the most powerful units on the market are the Hoover Concept One and Concept Two cleaners. Consumers should be aware that only the Concept One line is completely made in the USA. The four models range in price from $270 to to $370.

In addition to the Concept One line, Hoover makes more economically-priced cleaners. The 12 models in the Elite line replace the popular Convertible line. The Convertible vacuum cleaners have been America's best selling uprights for 30 years. The Elite cleaners retain the low prices ($90 to $160), but they have been improved with the addition of computer-designed motors. The units have automatic carpet level adjustment, easy-to-change disposable bags, and they are all light weight.

Hoover also makes cannister cleaners with

convenient attachments for vacuuming stairs, furniture, and other hard to reach places.

The Eureka Company prides itself on its reputation for quality. This reputation is well-earned—warranty returns for Eureka vacuum cleaners are less than one percent. Their latest innovation is the Freedom cleaner ($300), a battery-powered cordless upright assembled in Bloomington, Illinois. With this convenient and powerful vacuum, the days of tangled cords around table legs and interrupting cleaning to find another outlet are over. The rechargeable batteries allow the unit to operate for up to 30 minutes. The Freedom cordless upright is only one of 150 models in 15 different lines of vacuum cleaners the Eureka Company offers.

It has been ten years since **Black and Decker** introduced the revolutionary Dustbuster cordless hand vacuum, and today it is still America's best selling hand cleaner (it retails for $39). Black and Decker has since added a complete line of cordless hand cleaners. They include the new PowerPro Dustbuster Plus cleaners.

The PowerPro line of hand vacuums incorporates a more powerful motor to clean wet surfaces as well as dry. These cordless wonders can even take attachments for greater versatility. The top-of-the-line DB5000 Wet and Dry Vac ($83), for example, comes with two brush-attachments to clean surfaces from wet hardwood floors to hard-to-reach crevices inside your car.

In addition to cordless hand cleaners, Black and Decker has added two upright cordless vacuums. They are lightweight, run for about an average of 10-15 minutes when recharged, and are perfect for small cleaning jobs ($68 to $98). All of the company's cordless vacs come with a storage unit that also serves as a recharger.

Fans

Imported, inferior quality, ceiling fans are flooding the American market. We have heard consumers say: "a ceiling fan is a ceiling fan, they all blow the air around." Not true. A poorly made and designed ceiling fan can cause serious injury. The U.S. Consumer Product Safety Commission has recalled several models of cheap, imported fans, because they came with a ceiling fixture not adequate to hold the fan. In other words, an inferior fan can fall on your head, or your child's head. In addition, good quality fan motors will last a lifetime, while inferior ones will either do a poor job, or burn out in a few years.

Ceiling fans have been around for 100 years, but in the early 1970s they experienced a resurgence. In 1973 the **Casablanca Fan Company**, of Pasadena, California started manufacturing high-quality ceiling fans. Casablanca has made numerous improvements on the basic ceiling fan; recently it introduced "Inteli-Touch," an electronic switch which can alter fan speed and control a light from a simple two-wire connection. This allows fans to be installed without expensive re-wiring. The best Casablanca fans warrant the motor for life. Pull-switch operated Casablancas carry a ten-year warranty.

Fasco make high-quality ceiling fans in the United States. I have been using one for a year now and it works better that the other fans that I have installed. Its motor is durable and quiet, its blades sturdy and efficient, and its ceiling mount is substantial. All Fasco fans are made in the United States.

Emerson makes top-quality ceiling fans in Hazelwood, Missouri. This Emerson company is not related to Emerson Electric or Emerson Radio. All Emerson fans are made in the USA.

Another manufacturer of ceiling fans is **Hunter**. The best Hunter fans are manufactured in the United States. Their cheaper line of fans is made in Taiwan.

The **Vornado** fan combines the effectiveness of a ceiling fan with the advantage of portability. The Vornado fan, developed in the days before air conditioning in the 1940s, circulates air in a room more effectively than an ordinary fan. Fasco makes the heavy-duty motor contained in Vornado products.

Chapter Sixteen

Sporting Goods

America has always been a sports-oriented nation. Throughout the twentieth century organized sports, the NBA, NFL and Major League Baseball, have grown in popularity every year. Beginning in the 1970s, the fitness boom began as Americans of all ages and backgrounds became increasingly concerned about their health and appearance. Americans have begun to exercise as never before: running, swimming, bicycling and aerobics all enjoyed new levels of popularity. This, in conjunction with the plethora of softball leagues, bowling nights, golf, tennis and informal touch football leagues has turned America into a nation of sports fanatics.

It is no surprise, then, that the U.S. is a leader in technological advances and manufacturing of fitness products. Much of the finest personal and team sports equipment was invented and perfected in the USA.

Personal Exercise Equipment

In an image-concious society like that of the United States, there is an incredible demand for products that will improve appearance and health. Among the pioneers in the fitness industry are several U.S. based companies.

Nautilus has captured the imagination of those who desire a fitness system that works all parts of the body. The Nautilus workout is detailed and advanced. It incorporates such ideas as maintaining and improving a full range of muscular motion. Nautilus also advocates high repetitions with low weights to develop a muscle base. Nautilus has gradually phased-out products for the home. However, the use of Nautilus equipment in health clubs is quite common. These products appeal to a wide range of people. It is equally probable to find an accomplished athlete using this equipment, as it is to find an armchair quarterback doing the Nautilus workout.

Diversified Products (DP) and **Brutus by Excel,** also made in the USA, provide more basic and accessible products targeted for the home. From the basic bench press to a bench with both leg and arm accessories, DP and Brutus provide a blue-collar, free weight workout for those who wish to lift weights in their own home. DP also manufactures **Wynmor** fitness equipment for health clubs, which is more durable than its home equipment.

A DP Airgometer exercise bicycle is pictured above.

DP manufactures a number of high quality exercise bikes and treadmills too. The gem of this product line is the **AirGometer**. This product is made with dual action handlebars to combine an upper and lower body workout. The **AirGometer's** no impact workout is based on the principle that air resistance provides excellent cardiovascular conditioning. DP is one of the world's largest manufacturers of physical fitness equipment.

A combination of the advantages of free weights

and Nautilus can be found in the **Soloflex** machine. Soloflex is a machine for the home, similar to DP equipment. Unlike DP, Soloflex does not include weights. Instead, Soloflex provides a tension workout based on rubber straps that simulate real weights, but that work a wide range of muscular motion similar to the Nautilus. One is able to exercise without straining muscles by attempting to lift too much. A key advantage of the Soloflex is its versatility. The Soloflex can perform a range of exercises including bench presses, squats and curls. Soloflex can also be easily be adapted for curls and dips as well. Another advantage of this machine is its compactness; Soloflex can fit in an area as little as four foot square. Soloflex, which costs about $875 for the base unit, $150 each for the leg or butterfly extensions.

Another fitness system is **NordicTrack**, which simulates cross country skiing, shown above on the right. In addition to exercising all of the body's major muscle groups NordicTrack also develops cardiovascular fitness. Studies have shown that those who use this machine burns more calories per hour than rowing machines or exercise bikes, Ed Pauls, who invented the NordicTrack in 1975, founded the company in Chaska, Minnesota. The NordicTrack sells three different models, starting at about $500, which can be ordered by calling (800) 328-5888.

The NordicTrack is shown above.

Swimming

Speedo Swimwear is the best-known competitive swimming wear and equipment company in the United States, but some of its bathing suits, and all of its swim goggles are imported. **Tyr** of Huntington Beach, CA, makes all of its swimwear in the United States. Tyr drawstrings in men's suits are guaranteed not to come out. I have swum countless miles in a Tyr suit and it still looks new and the drawstring has remained in place. Tyr also makes women's swimsuits and baggy, noncompetitive bathing suits for men. Herman's Sporting Goods carries some Tyr suits. If you can't find a Tyr dealer call the company at (714) 897-0799.

The best swim goggles are made in America. The **Hind Compy**, made by Hind-Wells of San Luis Obispo, CA, has been worn by more record breaking competitive swimmers than any other goggle. I have just tried out a pair and they are terrific: they don't leak, they are comfortable and peripheral vision is excellent. According to competitive swimmers the Hind goggles' streamlined design reduce water drag. **Barracuda** goggles are also made in the USA and have won design awards. Goggles involve personal taste, you either hate or like a particular pair because of fit or looks.

After swimming try **Arena** shampoo which removes the chlorine from your hair. If you are interested in watersking, **O'Brien** makes top-quality water skis in the USA. O'Brien water skis are carried by L.L. Bean, (800) 221-4221.

A Tyr swimsuit is modeled above.

Baseball

Although baseball was invented in the United States, there are no baseballs made in the United States anymore. All of the large companies, including **Wilson, Rawlings** and especially **Spalding,** which claims to be "America's First Baseball Company," produce their baseballs in Haiti.

Finding a baseball glove made in the USA is almost as difficult as finding a baseball; there are only two major American manufacturers left. One company, **Nokona,** has maintained a commitment to making its products in the United States. Nokona is not a foreign name, but that of a Comanche Indian chief. Nokona makes a high quality glove for both baseball and softball. The company has resisted the temptation of high priced endorsements from major league players which allows them to keep their prices down. As their slogan says, "Nokona is as American as baseball." Nokona also manufactures one of the most unique products on the market: a glove made completely from kangaroo hide! This glove is made in the USA with Australian kangaroo hide. Nakona gloves are in the $100 to $150 price range.

Rawlings also makes some of its gloves in the United States. Their top-of-the-line glove, **Gold Glove** is made with "Heart of the Hide," leather made from the top five percent of the choicest American steers available; an exclusive, expensive tanning process is also used to help create a longer lasting and more durable glove. Rawlings Gold Glove is used by 58 percent of major league players, which range in price from $120 to $180.

The Rawlings Gold Glove is shown above.

The most advanced baseball bats are American-made. The traditional **Louisville Slugger** by Hillerich and Bradsby is made in the USA. The Louisville Slugger was developed to get Pete "The Gladiator" Browning out of a batting slump. Browning and "Bud" Hillerich created the first Louisville Slugger in Louisville in 1884. The first time Browning used the bat, he had three hits. This started a baseball tradition. Every year Hillerich and Bradsby turns 40,000 trees into about 1.4 million mostly white ash baseball bats. Hillerich and Bradsby started producing aluminum bats in 1978. Both the metal and wood bats are still made in the United States. Its Louisville Sluggers are exported to Japan and many other countries.

Easton Sports also offers a complete line of American-made bats. Easton specializes in aluminum and ceramic bats. From the Easton **Black Magic** to the **Ultra Light**, Easton makes bats for all levels of competition except professional. In fact, at the 1988 Olympics Team USA used Easton bats exclusively and 80 percent of the players at Seoul used their products. The newest addition to their product line is a composite bat made from fiberglass, graphite and ceramic.

Wiffle Balls and bats are made in America. They are ideal for playing baseball in your backyard because the danger of broken windows is reduced.

Basketball

Like baseball, basketball is a sport that is native to the United States. It is puzzling to learn that not a single basketball is made in the United States. There is one exception. **Wilson Sporting Goods** makes special-order basketballs—only for the government. Spalding makes the official basketball for the National Basketball Association in South Korea.

The **Schutt Manufacturing Company** makes all of its backboards in the United States. Schutt makes glass and aluminum boards for indoor and outdoor use. **Huffy Sports** (related to the bicycle company) is another maker of backboards. Huffy is the only manufacturer of backboards to carry the endorsement of the NBA. Huffy has tried to innovate in the staid backboard industry through the use of composites, graphics and its new elevator pole system.

Football

Wilson makes its Official National Football League ball in Ada, Ohio, where it produced the footballs for all Super Bowl games and every NFL game since 1941.

Official NFL footballs being made at the plant.

Gerry Cosby Company, located at Madison Square Garden in New York City, manufactures top quality shoulder pads for football players of all ages. Cosby shoulder pads ("The Professional's Choice") are the pads used by more than 350 of the players in the NFL, including Francisco 49ers star running back Roger Craig and all-pro linebacker Lawrence Taylor of the New York Giants. All Cosby pads are made in the United States. Cosby also makes an excellent line of equipment bags in the USA which are used by most of the pros.

Golf

Transplanted from the British Isles, golf is now established as a favorite sport in the United States. Nearly all types of golf equipment, including clubs, balls and shoes are made in the USA. **Wilson, Spalding, McGregor, Hillerich and Bradsby, Taylor, Ping** and even **Mizuno** make high-quality golf clubs in the United States.

Etonic makes golf shoes on the East Coast. **Reebok**, generally producing all of its shoes overseas, announced that it will produce golf shoes in the USA.

Titleist, Spalding and **Wilson** all produce golf balls in the United States. These balls include high quality balls that are often used on the professional tours.

Golf equipment made here is often exported to other countries where golf is popular, especially Japan, and a "Made in the USA" label has become a status symbol.

Tennis

An exception to the products made in the USA for individual sports is tennis racquets. Not a single tennis racquet is made in this country. Until recently Head made racquets here. However, they recently moved their manufacturing out of the country.

Tennis balls are still made in this country by **Wilson** and **Penn**. Wilson supplies balls for the U.S. Open, and it is a toss-up whether Wilson or Penn makes the best tennis balls.

Ice Skating

Riedell makes top quality hockey and figure skates in Redwing, MN (612) 388-8251. **Easton** and **Christian** make hockey sticks and **Vaughn** makes hockey pads in the U.S.

Bowling

Long popular with Americans, bowling is now being exported to the USSR. **Ebonite** and **Brunswick** make bowling balls in the United States and they are two of the most famous names. Brunswick is the world's largest manufacturer of bowling products. However, Ebonite claims more patents in the last decade than any other manufacturer.

Boxing

One can find both a grueling workout and a competitive sport in boxing. The world's most famous name in boxing equipment is **Everlast**. The company was the official supplier of boxing equipment for the 1984 Olympic Games in Los Angeles. The litany of champions that have used Everlast equipment is a veritable listing of boxing's greatest: Jack Dempsey, Rocky Marciano, Muhammad Ali, Marvelous Marvin Hagler.

All of Everlast's boxing equipment is made in the USA. A thumbless glove is also sold by the company. Recent research has shown that thumbless gloves reduce eye injuries, hand injuries, and facial lacerations. Everlast gloves retail for $38-$200, depending on the style and quality. The company also markets children's gloves which sell for less than $30. A complete selection of punching bags, uniforms, cups and headgear round out the Everlast boxing line of products.

It is also possible to purchase a full size boxing ring by mail from Everlast. Prices range from $8,800 for a plain elevated ring to $15,000 for an official Olympic ring. The serious boxer will use gloves and bags that are made in the USA. These products are also available for the home and provide an aggressive workout and a release for tension.

Volleyball

Centerline Sports makes "the last volleyball system you'll ever need." Their portable volleyball net, posts and stakes are functional and durable. They have two models which come in a special bag, which is included in the $150-$235 price. An optional sand kit, for setting up the system at the beach, is available. To order call (800) 451-3710.

Horseshoes

President Bush's favorite pastime is also one of the most American. The world's largest manufacturer of horseshoes, **St. Pierre**, is located in Worcester, Massachusetts. The company manufactures eight different models, all of which are approved by the National Horseshoe Pitching Association. St. Pierre horseshoes are 100 percent American, including the steel in the shoes.

Sportswear

One can also find the highest quality athletic wear in **Champion Sportswear** which is made in the United States. Champion's range of products is very wide and over 90 percent of its clothing is made in the USA. Most identifiable in the Champion line are the fleece sweatshirts and sweatpants. These products are extremely durable, yet become more comfortable with age. Champion also makes heavy-duty T-shirts and shorts, as well as other essential accessories.

Not only is this clothing well-suited for athletic activities, but Champion clothing has become fashionable as well. Fleece sweatshirts are a part of most college students' wardrobes and Champion has become the number-one line of athletic wear in Japan. Champion also exports to nineteen other countries. It is the number one seller in Italy and the number two seller in France.

Champion also makes uniforms for football, baseball, lacrosse and basketball in the United States. These uniforms are used at all levels of competition.

Russell makes top quality athletic wear, sweat shirts and pants in the United States. Russell clothing is available from L.L. Bean at (800) 221-4221.

Everlast, mentioned above for its boxing equipment, makes a full line of sweat pants and shirts for both adults and children.

Everlast athletic wear is shown above.

☆　☆　☆　☆　☆

Chapter Seventeen

Furniture

☆　☆　☆　☆　☆

The United States is blessed with an abundance of forests with a wide variety of furniture-quality wood. The United States actually has more trees growing now than it did seventy years ago because our timber companies plant more trees than they chop down. This is not the case in many parts of the world. If you buy a teak table from Denmark you are contributing to the decline of the world's rainforests.

The rosewood tree is nearly extinct from overcutting in Brazil. Teak is a major cash tree from the tropical rainforests in southeast Asia. Mahogany is grown in the rainforests of central America, and Africa and the Philippines. Zebrawood is grown in African rainforests.

Buying furniture made from American wood helps the American economy and the world environment at the save time, by preserving rainforests.

Examples of some of the fine quality wood which is grown in the United States:

American Wood

Pine
Oak (red and white)
Maple
Bird's Eye Maple
Walnut
Spruce
Birch
Beech
Aspen Poplar
Ash
Cedar
Cherry
Elm
Douglas Fir

Woods from the tropical rainforests of the world include:

Rainforest Imports

Teak
Mahogany
Ebony
Rosewood
Zebrawood

The rain forests of the world are a major source of medicine and other useful products and are being depleted at a horrifying pace. According to biologists nearly one-half of the species in the world live in these tropical rain forests. In addition rainforests take in carbon dioxide and release oxygen. This helps to counteract the "greenhouse" effect of carbon dioxide emissions from powerplants and automobiles.

The United States produces a wide variety of furniture, so diverse that we could write volumes about it. This chapter can only serve as a brief introduction to the best American furniture. American furniture styles range from Early American to modern, but also includes U.S.-made English, Italian, leather and "crate" styles.

The United States is blessed with an abundance of quality hardwood trees which form the backbone of the furniture industry. North Carolina is one principal furniture center, but Buffalo, New York and Grand Rapids, Michigan are also major furniture centers.

Early American Furniture

In 1885 in Buffalo, New York a new furniture company was born. It attracted new skilled immigrants from Poland, Germany and Italy and by 1913 became known as the Kittinger Furniture Company. Because of the quality of its products in 1937 the Williamsburg Foundation authorized Kittinger to be the exclusive manufacturer of **Williamsburg Foundation Furniture Reproductions.**

A Williamsburg "Lowboy" is shown above.

From 1969 to 1972 Kittinger was selected to refurbish the presidential offices in the West Wing of the White House. During that period the State Department gave Kittinger furniture as gifts to visiting dignitaries. The white damask fireside chairs that President Reagan sat in for many "photo opportunities" were produced in Buffalo.

Lane is one of the largest furniture manufacturers in the United States. It started out manufacturing cedar chests and became famous for them. Since turning its talents towards other furniture Lane has won the Daphne Award for design and use of wood. Lane produces more than 80 reproductions and adaptations of antiques approved by the Museum of American Folk Art. Shakers, who originated in England, live only in the United States, in small communities from Maine to Ohio, believe in common ownership of property and a strict and simple way of life. Their furniture style is plain and functional, distinctly different from the Williamsburg style.

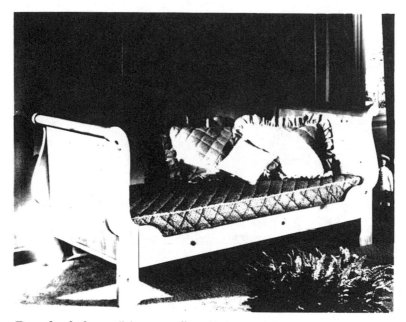

Day bed from "America" collection by Lane is shown.

Georgian Furniture

Georgian furniture was produced in the eighteenth century in England during the reigns of King George I to King George III. It is similar to some Early American furniture (especially Williamsburg) because it is the style of furniture many of the English immigrants were familiar with.

In addition to its Williamsburg line Kittinger also manufactures the **Georgian Collection.**

A Williamsburg piece is shown above.

One of the finest North Carolina furniture companies is **Drexel Heritage. Heirlooms** by Heritage is a collection of Georgian reproductions.

Another top manufacturer of Georgian reproductions is **Baker** of Grand Rapids, Michigan. Their
collections are copied from British antiques which were
selected by Sir Humphrey Wakefield, a noted antique
authority.

The **Bernhardt Furniture Company** of Lenoir, North
Carolina has over 50 hand-carved Georgian designs in
its **Centennial Collection.** These pieces are carved from
solid mohagany and other woods which demonstrate
careful attention to detail of the English originals.
Berhardt will send you a catalog or give you the name
of its nearest retailer. Call them at (704)758-9811.

Italian Furniture, Made in the USA

Old world craftsmen are alive and well in Brooklyn,
New York. **Casa Stradivari** manufactures furniture by

hand as it has done for four generations. It is still a family owned and operated business. All of its wooden furniture is glued and carved by hand, and then sanded, stained, hand-burnished, lacquered, rubbed with steel wool and finally polished into a work of art. Casa Stradivari can be reached at (212) 567-0195.

A Casa Stradivari chair is shown.

Contemporary American Furniture

Brayton International was born in 1973 to produce international design furniture in the USA. Brayton has won many design awards including the Roscoe Design Award and the Stuttgart Design Center Award. Its factory is in High Point, North Carolina, (919) 434-4151.

Stendig manufactures two unusual contemporary chairs in America, the **Nelson II** and the **Andover**. The stacking Nelson chair, made of Ash, was designed by Lindau and Lindekranz. The Andover was designed by Davis Allen of the architectural firm of Skidmore, Owings & Merrill. Stendig can be reached by calling (212) 838-6050.

Above is a loveseat and chair from Brayton.

Stendig chairs, Nelson II on the left and Andover on the right.

The Pace Collection manufactures desks, tables, cabinets and other high-quality contemporary furniture in the United States. Pace, like Stendig, manufactures many pieces in Europe as well. Pace furniture is very expensive. Their beautiful **Mezzaluna Executive Desk,** designed by Leon Rosen, is a half-moon shaped desk made out of polished stainless steel which sells for $20,000. The **K Desk,** designed by Steven Holl, is made out of Ash, and sells for $6,000.

Jack Lenor Larsen is another American furniture company which builds its products around the world, and sells them around the world. It has showrooms in eighteen countries in North America and Europe. American designer Ben Baldwin created the Baldwin Channel chair and couch and the **Cranbrook** lounge chair, which is available in a couch as well. Larsen headquarters are in New York City, (212) 674-3993.

The Pace K Desk is shown above.

A Baldwin Channel couch is pictured above.

R Jones & Associates is a relative newcomer to the furniture business, but its quality and style make it stand out. Its factory is located in Dallas, Texas, itself a new home to quality furniture manufacturing. R Jones produces more than 100 series of couches, loveseats and chairs and beds, and can be reached by calling (214) 951-0091.

Aristocrat Upholstery, of Bridgeport, Pennsylvania, also manufactures high-quality upholstered furniture. Most of its furniture is sectional, ideal for large living rooms. From gently curving pieces to rectangles, Aristocrat is an American manufacturer to look for when shopping for furniture. They can be reached at (215) 277-4500.

Mid-Priced, High-Quality Furniture

Thomasville and **Bassett** are two major manufacturers of mid-priced furniture. Both of these companies offer good value for the dollar, and provide a complete range of styles, from Early American to modern, from Chinese to country. For example a complete bedroom of Bassett furniture would range from $1000 to $2000, and Thomasville would be somewhat higher priced.

You Don't Have to Buy Italian
To Find High-Quality Leather Furniture

American companies manufacture fine leather furniture for every pocketbook. The **Brayton International Collection**, mentioned previously, also make top-end leather furniture. Brayton's Danube chair runs from $2,500 to $3,000 depending on the grade of leather selected. **Leathercraft** produces top-quality leather furniture in Conover, North Carolina, for less than half the price of Brayton International. Leathercraft can be reached at (704) 322-3305.

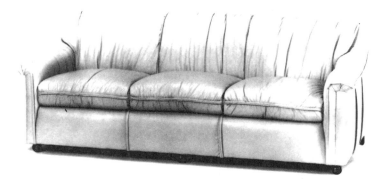

Above is a Leathercraft sofa.

Craftwork Guild and **Classic Leather**, both divisions of Vanguard Corporation, Hickory, North Carolina, manufacture leather furniture of good quality. Their furniture is slightly less expensive than that of Leathercraft. To find a store near you which carries these two lines call (704) 322-6365.

American Crate Furniture

In the last decade a new style of American furniture has arrived, "Crate Furniture." Several companies manufacture it, **This End Up, The Pine Factory** and **Cargo Furniture** among them. The first two are headquartered in the Richmond, Virginia area, Cargo in Ft. Worth, Texas. All of them have retail outlets in large areas of the United States.

Crate furniture is made out of solid pine and is reminiscent of wooden packing crates. It also is similar to Shaker furniture by being simple, durable and functional. Crate furniture is ideal for families with young children who need furniture that can take abuse. Prices are modest with a living room chair retailing for about $200-$250 and a couch for twice that.

To find a crate furniture retailer near you call one of the following toll-free numbers:

This End Up (800) 638-2234
Pine Factory (800) 433-7259
Cargo Furniture (800) 433-4018

Typical crate furniture bunk beds are shown above.

☆ ☆ ☆ ☆ ☆

Chapter Eighteen

Carpets and Rugs

☆ ☆ ☆ ☆ ☆

The American carpet industry is very healthy, the only significant imports are of Oriental rugs. And now one U.S. manufacturer, **Karastan**, has developed a computerized system for making Oriental-style rugs, in the United States. Another technological breakthrough in carpetmaking was made by Edward Fields in 1948 when the "Magic Needle" process was developed.

We will not take any position in the nylon versus wool "battle." There are advantages to both materials and there are quality manufacturers of both in the United States. Nylon carpeting dominates the market in the United States and there are virtually no nylon carpets imported into the U.S.

Quality Wool Carpets

Karastan produces more wool carpeting than any

other manufacturer in the United States. It produces broadloom and Oriental-style carpeting. To locate a retailer who carries Karastan products call (919) 665-4000.

Wool carpets are more expensive than nylon. Wool blends are priced in between. **Lanafil**, of Cohutta, Georgia, manufactures a wide range of wool and wool-blend carpets, ranging in price from $20 to $90 per square yard. To find a Lanafil retailer call (800) 252-1102.

Two other American producers of quality wool carpets are the **Carousel Carpet Co.**, of Ukiah, California, and the **Bloomsberg Carpet Co.**, of Bloomsberg, Pennsylvania. You can reach Carousel at (415) 863-3388 and Bloomsberg at (800) 336-5582.

Karastan Oriental-style Rugs

In the early 1970s a new system for fabricating multi-colored, patterned rugs was introduced by Karastan. This revolutionary system assembles, by computer, a pattern of various colors of yarn, which are brought together into a "cake" in which all yarns are parallel to each other, but assembled into the desired pattern. All patterns are computerized, and Karastan, in addition to Oriental patterns, makes **Garden of Eden** flowered patterns.

These Karastan rugs are all wool, and the patented process is only used by Karastan. The rugs come with a twenty-year warranty, and no rug has ever been returned to Karastan because of improper wear. The "Medallion Serapi" Oriental design carpet, shown on the next page, retails for about $800, much less than a similar carpet imported from Iran or Turkey.

Karastan Medallion Serapi design is shown.

Edward Fields Designs

Edward Fields developed a machine in the 1940s known as the "magic needle" which produces a "hand-made" carpet. A knowledgable operator is necessary to guide the machine, especially when a new pattern is being developed. Fields has more than 2,000 designs, the largest in the industry, in its library, and it can custom make any carpet that you can design.

Fields has produced rugs for the White House, but the firm will produce rugs for any interior designer. Their designs range from modern to whimsical, to conservative and everything in between. Bill Raiser, Field's first designer, also worked for industrial designer Raymond Loewy. New York artist Al Hirshfeld, and many other famous designers, have designs in the Field library. Fields' main office in New York City can be reached by dialing (212) 310-0400. A typical Fields all-wool rug sells for between $4,000 and $5,000 and retails for about $4,500 in a six by nine foot size.

Other Woven Wool Rugs

Woven rugs, like other types of carpeting, come in various qualities, but are generally more expensive and longer lasting. Hand-loomed woven rugs are still being produced by American Indians. Every one of these rugs is unique. In addition to hand-made woven rugs Wilton and axminster carpets are made in the USA. The Bloomsberg Carpet Company, mentioned previously, is the only manufacturer of Wilton rugs that we were able to locate in the U.S. Wilton carpets are machine woven loop carpets which can have intricate patterns, and are extremely long-lasting. Bloomsberg can be reached at (800) 336-5582.

An Edward Fields rug is shown above.

U.S. Axminster is the largest manufacturer of axminster carpets in the world. Most of their carpets are used in extremely high-traffic areas, like hotel lobbies and restaurants. Axminster carpets were patented in 1856 by a predecessor of U.S. Axminster. Axminsters can use unlimited numbers of colors, and many have fifty different colors, many more than Wiltons can have. U.S. primarily custom manufactures patterned axministers for commercial customers in wool and wool blends. However, also makes 14 different designs which are sold under the **Mohawk** name. Mohawk can be contacted at (800) 554-6637.

A U.S. Axminster carpet is pictured above.

Nylon Patterned Rugs

Not everyone can afford an Edward Fields' carpet. **Patcraft** in Dalton, Georgia ((404) 277-2133) produces a marvelous collection of machine made patterned carpets which cost a fraction of a Fields' masterpiece. Certainly, it is not wool and it is not custom-made, but there is a pattern that you will like.

Nylon Carpets

Ninety percent of the carpeting sold in the United States is made of nylon. Some top-line carpet manufacturers use only nylon, **Bigelow,** for example. Many carpet manufacturers use DuPont's **Stainmaster** carpet fibers. There are many different qualities of rugs made using the same fibers. Density of the fibers as well as the fibers themselves determines the quality and price of a piece of carpet. The more that a yard of carpet weighs the more fiber it contains and the more it will cost.

Almost all of the nylon carpeting sold in the U.S. is made in the USA. For this reason we will not recommend a specific brand of nylon carpeting only suggest that you carefully look at the pile and density and judge for yourself.

☆ ☆ ☆ ☆ ☆

Chapter Nineteen

American Beer and Wine

by Ben Giliberti

☆ ☆ ☆ ☆ ☆

The top American brewmeister, James Koch of Samuel Adams Boston Lager, said, "there was a time when people thought that Blue Nun was a great wine, just like there are people who think that Heineken and Beck's are great beers. In fact they are the Schlitz of Europe. They have a certain mystique, but it's a phony mystique." There is an American beer and wine for every palate.

The American market for beer and wine is the most open in the world. Canada refuses to allow beer brewed in the United States to be sold in its provinces; in contrast we accept Canadian brew with open arms. We charge a duty of 13 cents a case for imported beer. Holland, Germany and England charge us $2.93 a case for beer we sell there. China charges us a duty of $14 a case. Wine duties are similarly discriminatory against American products. To protest the unfair duties charged on American beer the Dock Street Brewery of Philadelphia has started a protest movement. Dock Street is putting labels on its bottles upside down until foreign duties are brought down to American levels. The Made in the USA Foundation has proposed that Congress raise duties on beer to equal the rate charged in the country exporting to America. Every time you order beer or wine think about the unfair treatment that we receive overseas and order American.

Great (and Good) American Beers

The growth of beer in America has in many respects paralleled the growth of the wine industry. Among the most exciting developments are the arrival within the last ten years of several dozen so called "micro-breweries," most all of which are wholeheartedly devoted to produce quality beers that can compete with the top offerings from Germany, Holland, England, Ireland and Belgium. Mass market American beers, most of which are heavily advertised, are well made and consistent, though they tend toward uniformity.

Many of these micro-breweries make their beers under contract with already existing breweries. Once the brand is established, however, many of these initially mom and pop operations graduate to their own facilities. Indeed, two of the finest producers, the Boston Brewing Company, the producer of Sam Adams beers, and New Amsterdam Beer started as contract breweries, but have since opened up their own breweries. Sam Adams is the only American beer which is sold in West Germany, which has exceptionally strict beer laws that some call "protectionist." The German "purity" laws prohibit beer with preservatives. However the Germans put preservatives in their export brews, including Beck's and St. Pauli Girl. James Koch says of the Boston Brewery, "beer has a shelf-life that's not a whole lot longer than orange juice. And you'd never think of buying orange juice from Germany. In Germany, they don't drink Beck's they drink the local brew."

Like the rest of the world's beers, American beers can be divided into two major types. Bottom fermenting beers, which include the familiar pilsener, ambers and bocks, are made from yeasts that settle to the bottom during fermentation. Top fermenting beers, which include ales, porters and stouts, are made from floating yeasts and tend to be fuller and heartier and deeper colored than bottom fermenters.

Though there are vast numbers of American beers worth trying, the following are my list of standouts, in order of quality. Given the quality, prices are extremely low, with most well under one dollar per 12 ounce bottle. The type of beer is indicated in parentheses.

Samuel Adams Boston Lager (amber, Massachusetts)
Sierra Nevada Pale Ale; Sierra Nevada Bigfoot (ale)
Anchor Steam Beer (amber, California)
Collin County Pure Gold (pilsener, Texas)
Boulder Extra Pale Ale (ale, Colorado)
Collin County Black Gold (boch, Texas)
Sierra Nevada Summerfest (amber, California)
Kessler Bock (bock, Montana)
Boulder Porter (porter, Colorado)
Dock Street Beer (Philadelphia)

New Amsterdam (amber, New York)
Sierra Nevada Stout (stout, California)
Kessler Lorelei (pilsener, Montana)
Cold Spring Export (pilsener, Minnesota)
Anchor Porter (porter, California)
Rhomberg Classic Pale Ale (ale, Iowa)

Among the larger volume producers, here are the standouts:

Augsberger (Wisconsin)
Erlanger's (Owned by Strohs)
Stroh's Signature
Michelob (Anheuser-Busch)

American Wine

Virtually all American wines have European counterparts made from the same grape varieties with many or all of the same classic flavors. If you understand the wine regions of Europe, finding an American counterpart with similar classic varietal characteristics is a simple matter.

But bear in mind that "counterpart" does not mean "clone," and "similar" hardly means "identical." A California cabernet may be made from the same grapes as a sturdy French Medoc, but each has its own special strengths. Understanding these differences as well as the similarities can open up a whole new world of wine appreciation for all who enjoy great wine. And in many cases, the American alternative is less expensive and offers better value.

The focus of this chapter will be on the best American wines in each category, for that is where a country earns its reputation for greatness. Mention will also be made of less costly examples of these same varieties of wines, for that is where a country develops its reputation for value. To be sure, America offers a wine for every palate and every pocketbook.

Cabernet Sauvignon

In recent years sophisticated wine drinkers have come to know "cigar box" aromas from Pauillac, leather and tobacco tastes from Grave, spicey perfume from Marguax and the distinctive *gout de terroir* ("taste of the soil") of the other great Bordeaux regions. But nowadays, with the dollar/franc equation more in their favor, California's top vintners are hoping for a rediscovery of the distinctive flavors of America's own great cabernets.

The term "Rutherford dust" was coined by the legendary winemaker Andre Tchelistcheff, the architect of the great Beaulieu George de Latour Private Reserve cabernets, to characterize the spicey, minty and Eucalyptus-like flavors and aromas of the cabernets products on what may be America's most distinguished vineyard area, the Rutherford Bench. As a meaningful tasting term, "Rutherford dust" has been damned as much as praised. But at least it highlights what almost everyone seems to admit: The Bench is special.

Nowhere is the gathering of America's cabernet elite more conspicuously in evidence than on this four mile stretch of gravelly loam in the heart of Napa. With every step along Highway 29, Napa's famous tourist wine road that separates the Bench from the rest of the valley, one seems to come upon another member of California's cabernet aristocracy. **Beaulieu George de Latour Private Reserve; Robert Mondavi Reserve; Heitz Martha's Vineyard; Freemark Abbey Bosche; the**

Inglenook Reserve Cask Cabernets; and most recently, **Rubicon,** from the **Niebaum-Coppola** vineyard.

What's special here is the soil. The Bench soil lends an extra dimension—the sense of place and the taste of the soil—that comes through in wine from a specific *terroir* ("microclimate"). The Bench's magnificent profusion of superb cabernets from vineyards in close quarters provides an opportunity that is truly rare: the chance to explore the interplay of soil and winemaking in determining the greatness and character of wine.

Perhaps the most famous single American vineyard is Martha's Vineyard, which hugs the foothills of the Mayacamas Mountains, far back from the route 29 highway. The crusty Joe Heitz has made the wine here since 1966, and the **Heitz 1984 Martha's Vineyard** ($35) displays every bit of the famous, some might say notorious, Martha's Vineyard eucalyptus and mint bouquet. Very ripe and loaded with tannin, this is one to lay down.

Martha's knarled old cabernet vines came initially from cuttings from two tiny experimental plots superbly positioned between Martha's Vineyard and the **Robert Mondavi Reserve** vineyards. The property of the U.C. Davis wine school, the two experimental vineyards also supplied the grapes for the **1985 Long Cabernet Sauvignon** ($30). Though still young and massive, it may be among the finest wines of the vintage.

The 1985 Long surely faces stiff competition from the **1985 Robert Mondavi Reserve** ($20-25). Though slightly lighter than the Long, the Mondavi is a classic Rutherford cabernet, with warm, fleshy fruit and round tannins. More classically structured, with deep, sculptured fruit is the suave **1985 Far Niente** ($25), a first growth quality wine from an emerging superstar next door to Mondavi.

Moving north past the Robert Mondavi winery, the Bench soil remains the same, but a gentle warming trend occurs, yielding, at least in theory, slightly richer wines. At this point of the Bench a bold revival is underway. Napa pioneer Gustave Niebaum's three principal vineyards, which produced the great pre- and post-prohibition **Inglenook Reserve Cask cabernets**, are once again producing wine as fine as any in Napa.

From the former Niebaum "estate" vineyard, far back toward the foothills, film maker Francis Ford Coppola has directed the production of the stunning **1982 Rubicon** ($34), a massive, black, richly flavored cabernet sauvignon and cabernet franc blend with tremendous aging potential. From directly in front of the Inglenook winery, the richer, less gravelly soil of the Inglenook Ranch vineyard has supplied most of the cepage for the **1984 Inglenook Reserve Cask Cabernet** ($12-15). This supple, minty, very fruity offering, has become one of California's hottest cabernets since its medal winning performance at a recent California Wine Experience. The **1983 Inglenook Reunion Cabernet** for the first time in twenty years combined production from Niebaum-Copolla, Inglenook Ranch and Napanook, Niebaum's third major vineyard, to the south near Yountville, duplicating the blend of the legendary Inglenooks of the past.

Those who question the aging ability of California cabernets need only experience the cabernets produced since 1936 on the DePins vineyard north of the present and former Inglenook properties. The **Beaulieu George Latour Private Reserve 1985** ($20), produced from De Pins is a totally different wine from the Inglenook, much oakier and backward, but with a more classic structure—more like Bordeaux.

What a contrast to the quintessentially Californian

Freemark Abbey 1985 Bosche ($24). Experts have rated the Bosche vineyard, adjacent to DePins, among the very best of Napa.

Nowhere is that more true than in the case of the the Martha's Vineyard dead ringer **1986 Johnson-Turnbull Cabernet** ($17), as eucalyptus-like as anyone could want, at far less money than the Heitz offering. Particularly fine also is the **Cakebread Cellars 1986 Cabernet** ($17), produced next door to Johnson-Turnbull. No mintiness here, but instead, delicate, pure fruit and a sweet bouquet that calls to mind a well-made young Margaux. Honorable mentions must also go to the delicious, spicey **1985 Sequoia Grove** ($12); the well-made, but closed in **1984 Flora Springs** ($12); and the very lush and deep **Robert Pepi 1984 "Vine Hill Ranch"** ($14). Best buy honors go to **Franciscan 1985 Estate Cabernet** ($7-9).

Chardonnay, The American White Burgundy

Frenchman Michel Laroche admits that he has lately become an unabashed admirer of a California chardonnay. That might not be notable were Laroche not also the owner of Domaine Laroche, one of France's leading producers of grand cru chablis. The chardonnay is from the Les Pierres vineyard and is made by what may be the the the Golden State's hottest winery, Sonoma Cutrer. Many have likened the style of Sonoma Cutrer to that of grand cru chablis and other premium white burgundies, all of which are made from the chardonnay.

Laroche approves of **Sonoma Cutrer's** blend of traditional and modern methods. Some techniques, like use of the cooling tunnel, merely duplicate the natural cooling effects of Chablis' northerly climate, he said.

Others represent advances that he is considering instituting himself. Laroche says Sonoma Cutrer has what he looks for in a great wine—balance. Sonoma Cutrer, has acidity balanced with fruit "in a more austere, French style," he said.

Laroche firmly believes that there is a market for American wines like Sonoma Cutrer in France. Laroche regularly uses Sonoma Cutrer as the mystery wine in his blind tastings. He reported that his tasters, who are not only confounded most of time, were very impressed.

Of recent vintages, the **1985 Les Pierres** ($19 retail) is extraordinary, but the recent **1986 Cutrer** ($19) and **1987 Russian River** ($13) bottlings are also of high quality. The Les Pierres should be aged for several years, and the others can also benefit from aging.

Some of the best chardonnays:

Matanzas Creek "Sonoma County" 1985/86 ($15): Topflight, perfumed, appley bouquet. Very concentrated, exuberant fresh fruit flavors lightly seasoned with vanilla oak. Superb efforts that will improve for a year or more, but delightful now. The fine 1986 is more open and more ready now.

La Crema Reserve 1986 (California; $17): Captivating spicey, powerful new oak bouquet. On the palate, full fruit flavors overlayed with very toasty oak and buttery notes. French style chardonnay that is ready to drink now.

Burgess Cellars Vintage Reserve 1986 (Napa; $10-11): Worthy successor to the fine 1985. Recalls a good Mersault. Intriguing earthy, burgundian nose. Much toasty oak and complex fruit on the palate.

Beaulieu Los Carneros Reserve 1986 (Napa; $11-13): Fully realizing the potential of its superb Carneros vineyards, Beaulieu has given us this marvelously complex, refined chardonnay loaded with soft fruit, and with a long finish. A charmer.

Pine Ridge Knollside Cuvee 1986 (Napa; $13-14) Exceedingly well-made, distinctive smoky bouquet and intriguing gingery notes on the palate. Excellent for current drinking.

Beringer Napa Valley 1986 ($10-$12): Tasted against the finest chardonnays, this 40 percent barrel fermented wine didn't betray its modest price in the least. Spicy, yeasty bouquet. Well structured, savory fruit and lively acidity. Long finish. Definite short-term aging potential.

William Hill Reserve 1986 (Napa; $13-18;): Refined, complex, understated style of chardonnay with the balance to age well. One or more years cellaring suggested.

Kalin Cellars Cuvee LV 1985 ($18): Attractive, yeasty, citrus nose. Tangy style on the palate, long finish.

Raymond Napa Valley 1986 ($12): Effusive vanilla and citrus bouquet, rich, buttery style. Impressive effort that harkens back to full-bodied style of the not too-distant past.

Clos Du Bois Proprietor's Reserve 1986 (Alexander Valley, $25-30): Fine ripe style with well integrated fruit and vanilla oak.

Hanna 1987 (Sonoma, $15): Pleasing vanilla and apple notes in bouquet. Copious, forward, fruit jumps out on the palate; light oak notes.

Hacienda Clair de Lune 1987 (Sonoma, $12): Sweet oak, floral bouquet, complex mineral, lemony, spicey flavors in a subtle lighter style; crisp finish. Fine wine, fine value.

Saintsbury Carneros 1986 ($12-13): Restrained, medium body on palate, earthy burgundian nose; skillful integration of fruit and oak flavors; French in style; confirms Saintsbury's position, a versatile match with most foods.

Monticello Corley Reserve 1987 (Napa, $13-14): Still tight, but plenty of pure, complex fruit behind the structure. Well-made.

Mazzocco Vineyards 1986 (Sonoma, $12): Extroverted style; heavy toasted oak; well constituted with a full flavor.

De Loach Russian River 1987 ($13): Pineapple, citrus nose. Very full, almost thick flavors. Strong finish.

Sanford Santa Rosa County 1985 ($15): Very ripe, butterscotch nose, full rich style on palate. Fully mature.

Fetzer Sundial 1987 (California, $8-9): A full-flavored, fresh style of chardonnay from one of the California's most reliable mid-priced wineries.

Kendall-Jackson Proprietor's Reserve 1986 (California, $25): Nice touch of oak, appley fruit, slightly low acidity. The less pricey **Vintner's Reserve** ($9-10) offers good value.

Callaway Calla-Lees 1987 (Temecula, $9-10): Yeasty bouquet, cleanly made, crisp, lively style, distinctive in that it sees no oak aging, but is left for an extended period on the lees after fermentation.

Prince Michel Barrel Select 1986 (Virginia, $18): Thrown in as a ringer in the blind tasting, held its own in some fine company. Aromatic, with good, tart acidity and excellent varietal flavor, will shock those who dismiss Virginia wines as mere curiosities.

St. Francis 1986 (Sonoma, $9.50): Exotic, very ripe fruit, butterscotch notes; loose-knit structure, good for near- term drinking.

Wente Arroyo Seco Reserve 1985 (Livermore, $10): Rich, herbal bouquet and full, soft, buttery flavors. Solid value.

Concannon Selected Vineyard 1985 (Santa Clara and Santa Maria, $9): Interesting caramel and buttery aromas and flavors, but a bit tart in the finish. By the way, if you see a bottle of this winery's superb, powerful '84 or '85 sauvignon blanc ($9), grab it.

Champagne and Sparkling Wines

For many wine drinkers, it's French champagne—or settling for second best. Savvy wine consumers are putting this "accept no substitutes" point of view aside and trying the worthiest challengers from the U.S.

Many of the best new releases from California are priced below the level of French champagne. The line between French and American champagne is beginning to blur. In recent years, leading French champagne houses have invested heavily in the United States, setting up shop with wineries and vineyards in Napa, Carneros, Anderson Valley, and elsewhere in the Golden State. The progeny which include Domaine Mumm, Roederer Estate, Maison Deutz, Piper Sonoma and Domaine Chandon, stack up quite well against their parents.

One California-French hybrid that can surely hold its own with the worlds's best is **Roederer Estate**. It's a dead ringer for French champagne. Roederer Estate's fruit is from the Anderson Valley.

Compared to California sparklers, French champagnes show a more pronounced yeasty, biscuity, and toasty flavors. Most California sparkling wines display more fruit. The high fruit levels may be California's greatest asset. Such wines are very forward and need no additional aging to show their best.

The following champagnes are recommended:

Roederer Estate Brut ($14, Anderson Valley): Small

bubbles, toasty, biscuity flavors, lots of finesse, and a hint of bright grapiness that should have, but didn't, tip me off that this was Californian. Superb. Very highly recommended.

Iron Horse Blanc de Blancs 1984 ($24, Sonoma County, Green Valley): Pleasing, apple-like bouquet, and beautifully expressed, generous chardonnay fruit overlaid by the light, tiny bubbles.   Highly recommended.

Mumm Cuvee Napa Brut Prestige ($14; Napa): Pinkish tinge and strawberry-, red burgundy-like nose reflects heavy employment of pinot noir in the cepage. Because of its high fruit level, this was least champagne-like of all the California-French offspring, but it was still well-made and pleasant. Recommended.

Gloria Ferrer Brut ($10-$12, Napa): Active, frothy mousse; fine, mineral scented, chardonnay nose. Solid, firm and lively on the palate. Highly recommended, a best buy.

Maison Deutz Brut ($15, Santa Barbara): Very active mousse; austere, taut, champagne-like structure

Domaine Chandon Brut (Moet) ($12, Napa): Very French-styled, in a lean, elegant style. And don't miss the tasty Domaine Chandon Reserve ($19).

Piper Sonoma Brut ($14): Fine smoky bouquet. On the palate, full, pinot noir dominated flavors with a nice vanilla note.

Scharffenberger 1984 Blanc de Blancs Brut ($18, Mendocino): Pleasantly fruity, almost grapy, but lacks the excitement of the top offerings.

Pinot Noir/Red Burgundy

French red burgundy is a great wine. The problem is, there has never been enough of it, at least at prices most of us can afford.

Despite some early failures, American pinot noir is increasingly proving itself to be as high in quality as all but a handful of top French Burgundies. In California, the most consistent results have come from the more temperate Carneros region straddling Napa and Sonoma, where the best wines are truly Burgundian in character.

Oregon, however, with long summer days and a northerly climate, may prove to be the true American home for the pinot noir. Its ever-improving reputation traces back to 1979, when French experts picked a 1975 Eyrie Vineyards pinot noir over several famous French burgundies at a Paris tasting. Many Oregon offerings will remind burgundy fans of a good Volnay or Beaune. The following clearly stood out:

Saintsbury 1986 Carneros (California, $11-13): Immensely fruity bouquet, clean, vibrant pinot noir fruit, with moderate tannins and classic burgundian expansion of the palate. Superb value.

Santa Cruz Mountain Vineyards 1985 (California, $15-18): Good winemaking is evident in this rich, chewey, pinot. Should you taste a bit of Pauillac or Cote Rotie in these wines, however, you'll understand my sole reservation about winemaker Ken Burnap's efforts here.

Oak Knoll 1986 Vintage Select (Oregon, $14): A smoky, cherry bouquet, silky, elegant fruit and firm tannins make this an ideal pinot noir for drining and enjoying now.

Bethel Heights Willamette 1985 (Oregon, $12): Deep purple color and lush, lively raspberry fruit, and long, mouthfilling finish.

Robert Mondavi 1984 Reserve (California, $16-18): The smoky, toasty oak provides a fine counterpoint to the pure pinot fruit of this offering.

Hacienda 1985 (California, $12-14) Nicely defined structure, and well-balanced, complex fruit.

Soleterra 1985 (California, $14): Ripe, earthy firmly-structured and tannic style. Not particularly burgundian, but a good wine at the price.

Light Fruity Style Wines—Red Zinfandel

In search of red wines for summer drinking, American wine consumers have traditionally looked to Europe rather than to our own vineyards for light, fruity and refreshing reds than can be served chilled on a hot summer day.

All but overlooked in the search have been the reds produced from that quintessentially American grape, the zinfandel. That's a shame, because when it is made in a lighter style, zinfandel can be a superb summer red, delivering generous dollops of fresh raspberry-like fruit, along with enough structure to stand up to tangy summer salads and charcoal-grilled foods. In addition, at prices as low as $4 to $5 a bottle, zinfandel represents outstanding value.

To those unfamiliar with its many incarnations, however, zinfandel may at first seem an unlikely choice for a summer red. One rather fundamental reason is that many wine consumers may be surprised to discover that red zinfandel exists at all. A whole generation of wine drinkers is more familiar which white zinfandel, which is made by fermenting ordinary red zinfandel grapes off their deeply pigmented skins to minimize color extraction. White zinfandel, which is really a rosé, or blush wine, has achieved enormous commercial success, but to date little of its success has rubbed off on its red cousin, which remains a relatively slow seller compared to cabernet and merlot.

Those who try a lighter red zinfandel will find that it neatly bridges the gap between the more familiar types of zinfandel. It maintains most all of the spicey, refreshing notes that have made white zinfandel such a hit, but unlike most white zinfandels, it is fully dry and usually more complex. It also captures much of the explosive fruit of the bigger zinfandels, but its lower alcohol, lighter color, and less aggressive character make it a far better choice for summer drinking.

In an era when the top Beaujolais are fetching $12 or more per bottle, zinfandel captures the original spirit of Beaujolais even better than many true French Beaujolais.

By contrast, the summer zinfandels seek only to deliver lots of fresh, grapy pleasure at a modest price. In this regard, they succeed splendidly. The following are my choices, listed in order of preference:

Ravenswood 1987 Vintners Blend ($7): Superb; bursts with wealth of raspberry fruit; harmonious balance between fruit and moderate tannins; intense without ever seeming heavy.

Parducci Mendocino County 1986 ($6): Brilliant ruby color. Vibrant, light picnic style zinfandel, with fresh strawberry notes on bouquet and palate, and a crisp, clean finish.

Guenoc Lake County 1985 ($7): Spicy, elegant, claret style zinfandel with fruit that is both lush and well focused.

Sebastiani Sonoma County 1986 ($5-6): A real bargain; soft, grapy fruit, light quaffing style perfect for patio sipping.

Beringer North Coast 1986 ($8): Medium weight, claret style with fine complexity; impressive depth of flavor. **Karly Amador County 1987** ($8): Outstanding depth and exuberant expression of fruit. Drink now for grapy fruit, but hold some for mellower pleasures this fall.

Kendall-Jackson Mendocino 1986 ($7): Though not necessarily the best of Kendall-Jackson's stable of excellent zinfandels, clearly the freshest and grapiest, with some earthiness on the nose.

Pedroncelli Sonoma County 1986 ($7): As always, good value is offered by Pedroncelli in this light to medium weight offering featuring ripe round fruit and a smooth finish.

Seghesio 1985 Northern Sonoma 1985 ($6): A pleasing, lighter style; crisp and mature.

Fetzer California 1986 ($6): Light to medium weight, clean strawberry flavors nicely set off by American oak notes.

Marietta Old Vines Red Lot 7 (non-vintage, $5-6): More muscular and dense than the fabulously successful Lot 6 offered last year. Still offers a good value, although the addition of petite sirah detracts from the former sprightliness of the wine.

Rosés and White Zinfandels

As the accompaniment to a light summer meal served after a hot day, few wines can match the refreshing appeal of a lightly chilled rosé. Their pink to salmon color suggests how perfectly they fill the gap between reds, most of which are too heavy in summer, and whites, which lack the body to match many dishes.

The top American rosés offer a surprisingly high level of quality, complexity and value. Many can compete head to head in flavor with the best French rosés, and prices are modest, often well under $10. The best Rosés:

Bonny Doon's Vin Gris de Cigare, produced in California by the colorful Randall Graham, is one such wine. Made from the tradional Rhone grape varieties in a bone dry format, the inspiration for this wine is the dry rosés made near the French village of Chateauneuf du Pape.

Bonny Doon's label may be the most distinctive ever stuck on a wine bottle. It's a reverse affair that can only be seen by looking through the wine. It depicts a peaceful vineyard scene—with a flying saucer hovering overhead. The inspiration for the flying saucers (*Cigare volant*) is a Chateauneuf du Pape village ordinance banning such conveyances from the skies above its vineyards.

Vintages hardly matter with rosés. Drink them as young as possible. They rarely improve with age. The 1986s and 1987s are at the peak. Most '85s are also fine.

Bonny Doon 1988 Vin Gris de Cigare ($9): Made primarily from the mourvedre, the major grape of Bandol, this one is too good and too much fun to pass up. The fruit is light and expansive on the palate, with light peach and orange notes; it has the length to prove that rosés really can have a finish. The first great American rosé, and arguably the tastiest rosé made.

Heitz Grignolino Rosé 1986 ($6): This may be the Martha's Vineyard of rosé; lots of spicey, gewurtztraminer-like character in the nose and on the palate.

Amador Foothills 1988 White Zinfandel ($7): Bone dry, yet loaded with fresh, strawberry-like fruit. A real gem.

Beringer 1988 White Zinfandel ($8): A huge seller, and its not hard to see why. Spicey fruity, with loads of charm.

The Challenge of American Winemaking

Having discussed American wines by grape variety, it is also important to understand what goes into American wines besides grapes. For although American wines are made from European varietals, there is a boldness to them that is distinctly American. While surely this has much to do with climate and winemaking techniques, in my view, this character has less to do with these factors than with something else, more abstract perhaps, but no less critical—the simple determination to succeed, combined with that most American of virtues—ingenuity. By all the criteria that the experts have established as necessities for great wine, for example, proper soil types, climate and grape varieties, high quality American wine should be an impossibility.

That America is not a natural breeding ground for the production of great wine might come as a shock to many of us. In some quarters, we have been led to believe that America is a winemaker's Nirvana. We are told that in California, every year is a vintage year; that the French send their winemakers here to study in our schools; that American wines consistently win in blind tastings against their European competitor.

Let's start with climate. Compared with the relatively moderate climates of Bordeaux, Burgundy, northern Italy and even of Spain, the American climate looks like an obstacle course. It's too hot. The growing season is too short. The day/night temperature variation is too great. It's either too damp, as in Maryland, Virginia and Oregon, or it's a virtual desert, as in Napa and Sonoma.

To be sure, some of these conditions are great for producing tanker loads of jug wines for mass consump-

tion, as Franzia and Gallo have shown in California's
Central Valley. However, such climatic extremes are
anathema to great wine.

To beat the heat, the California's vignerons have
been particularly resourceful. In Napa, former American Airlines pilot turned winemaker, Tom Burgess,
was among the first to move up the Valley's eastern
slopes in search of cooler temperatures that would
allow for the slower ripening so essential to the complex chemistry of great wines. Today, almost two decades later, several of Burgess' early hillside vintages
are still aging gracefully in the bottle. More recently,
in the Stag's Leap area, the high quality of **Shafer Hillside Select, William Hill Reserve, Pine Ridge** and other
hillside cabernets and chardonnays have further proved
the wisdom of higher elevation plantings.

Those who have chosen to stay on the valley floor
have not been left behind, however. Among the innovators here is the **Robert Mondavi** winery, which along
with the Baron Philippe de Rothschild, has introduced
Opus One. Though sometimes categorized as a luxury
item, Opus One is in fact a bold, pioneering effort in
the use of canopy management—allowing the grape
leaves themselves to provide shade for the hanging
bunches—to control the scorching, direct California
sunlight. While the jury is not yet in on the aging
ability of Opus One, the recently released 1985 appears
to have all the components to challenge the Bordeaux
first growths in all respects save price—where the Opus
is in fact less costly.

Perhaps the first to realize the limitations of our
own varietals was Thomas Jefferson, who believed that
palatable wines were an essential ingredient of a popular democracy. On his return from a stint in France as
the American Minister of trade, Jefferson swapped

native American trees and plants—then very much the rage in European botanical gardens—for cuttings of vines from Europe's finest vineyards, including Le Montrachet, Chateau Margaux and those of the Italian Piedmont.

Although Jefferson own viticultural experiments in Virginia failed, there's no question who ultimately got the better of the deal. Two centuries later, American cabernet sauvignons decisively outpointed the top French Bordeaux in a challenge tasting put on by the French winemakers, known as the "Judgment of Paris" tasting. By contrast, the American plants sent to Europe carried in their roots the dreaded phylloxera louse, which devastated the European vineyards. All European varieties must be grafted on to phylloxera-resistant American rootstock.

Innovation continues in East Coast vineyards as well. Little more than a decade ago, commercial winemaking barely existed in Virginia, Maryland and Pennsylvania, where they are still battling the same problems that appear to have undone Jefferson's early efforts—humidity-induced rot in the summer, and sudden vine splitting cold snaps in the early spring.

To battle the winter chills, many local wineries have turned to winter-hearty hybrids with great success. Excellent hybrid bottlings included the crisp seyval blanc produced by Virginia's **Oakencroft Winery**, a toastier, woodier verson of the same grape offered by Maryland's **Montbray Vineyards**, and the seyval blanc, vidal blanc blend put out by Pennsylvania's **Chaddsford Winery**, called **Chaddsford White**, a legitimate bargain at around $6. With regard to vinifera plantings, more careful site selection has helped to improve the odds against freezing. Examples of highly successful vinifera bottlings include recent vintages of the impressive

Prince Michel Vineyards Barrel Fermented chardonnay and **Montdomaine Cellar's** cabernet and merlot blends.

But ingenuity and pluck are one thing. Taste is quite another. Have all these qualities given our wines a distinctively American flavor?

To my palate, they have. If there is one single characteristic that sets American wine apart from the wines of Europe, it is their boldness. American chardonnays burst with a clean fruit that would almost be embarrassing in a white Burgundy. Our cabernets won the *Judgment of Paris* tasting by making their French counterparts look like black and white renditions. I can't help but feel this boldness reflects the bold ingenuity of our winemakers—and I sure like the taste of it in our wines.

Value in American Wines

What also must be appreciated is the value offered by American wines. Are American wines underpriced? At least one well-known winemaker, Diamond Creek Winery owner Al Brounstein, says the answer is yes. He priced **1987 Diamond Creek Lake Vineyard Cabernet** will carry at a $100 retail price, the highest ever attached to a newly minted American wine.

Maintaining that other top wineries have underpriced their offerings compared with other world class competitors, such as Chateau Petrus and the Domaine de la Romanee Conti, Brounstein predicts that other American vintners will soon follow his lead. Other worthy $100 a bottle candidates include Dunn Howell Mountain, Stag's Leap Cask 23 and Grace Family Vineyards, all of which sell for between $25 and $40 a bottle, as well as others, he said.

The good news for consumers is that even if Brounstein is correct, the wines he refers to represent but a tiny portion of California's premium wine production. The Lake bottling is itself a prime example. It comes from a tiny 3/4 acre vineyard near the winery. Though as many as 200 cases are produced in abundant years, only 75 cases were produced in 1987. Because of its cool micro-climate, the vineyard's production is sold separately only in exceptionally hot years, which produce the best wine there. The most recent Lake bottling was 1984, and the only previous vintage was 1978. It has already been decided that there will be no 1988 Lake bottling.

The message is clear, however. Since prices can only head one way—up—this is a propitious moment to stock the cellar with high quality American wines. They deserve a place in any cellar that is devoted to quality wine.

☆ ☆ ☆ ☆ ☆

Chapter Twenty

American Food

☆ ☆ ☆ ☆ ☆

American food products are more abundant and diverse than from any other country in the world. And American produce contains less dangerous pesticides than fruits and vegetables from other countries. For example, DDT was banned in the USA, but is now imported into this country on foreign tomatoes and other produce.

The climate of the USA varies dramatically from Alaska to Hawaii and from Maine to California, with each region having its own best fruits, vegetables, meat and fish. U.S. food products known around the world range from Heinz Ketchup and McDonalds all-American beef hamburgers, to smoked salmon and Maine lobster. This chapter cannot possibly cover every high-quality American food product, but merely seeks to expose you to the highlights of American food.

Bottled Water

The most ridiculous import of all is bottled water. Think of the wasted fuel alone that it takes to ship water from Europe to the United States. Perrier, that snobby beverage from the South of France, was dethroned in the US last year because it was found to be contaminated with benzene. This caused a recall of the French bubbly, and introduced hundreds of thousands of Americans to **Quibell** and **Saratoga** bottled water. Don't think about ordering Perrier, or Evian, when American carbonated water tastes just as good, for a lower price.

American Coffee

Coffee beans are grown on two American islands, Hawaii and Puerto Rico. Hawaii's **Kona Coffee** is grown on the lush volcanic slopes of the Kona coast. You can order Kona Coffee from Mauna Loa at (800) 832-9993 for $15 for half a pound. Puerto Rican coffee is more abundant and less expensive. **Cafe Jaucano** and **Cafe Rico** can be found at coffee stores.

American Vegetables

Five very important vegetables originated in America, and are now cultivated around the world: tomatoes, corn, peppers, eggplant and potatoes. Can you imagine Ireland without the potato, or Italy without tomatoes? The most American vegetable is corn, which Americans eat on the cob, and which is the source of the great American snack, popcorn. Avocados are also native to America and were not introduced into Europe until the 20th century.

A short list of some of the best American vegetables:

New Jersey Beefsteak Tomatoes
Idaho Potatoes
Silver Queen Corn (various states)
California Artichokes
California Avocados

American Fruits and Nuts

Florida Grapefruit
Hawaiian Pineapple
Macadamia Nuts (Hawaii)
Washington State Apples
Oregon Pears
Georgia Peaches
Nubiana and Santa Rosa Plums (California)
Pecans (Georgia)
Almonds (California)
Pistachios (California)
Cranberries (Massachusetts)
Blueberries (Maine)
Cherries (Michigan)
Pears (Oregon)

The California products listed above are all available from California Cachet in San Francisco at (800) 422-2438 or (415) 777-1000. In addition to fruit and nuts, California Cachet carries a wide variety of California wines and will ship anywhere in the world.

You can order pecans and peaches from Melatchie Farms, Perry, Georgia at (800) 241-7013 and from Orchard Pecan, Albany, Georgia at (800) 841-4350. Pecans are the only nut native to North America. Blueberries are available from the Maine Wild Blueberry Co., Machias, Maine, at (800) 243-4005. Florida grapefruits will be shipped worldwide by Indian River Citrus Specialties, direct from their groves, (800) 223-7740. Pinnacle Orchards in Medford, Oregon, sells its pears around the world, (800) 547-0227.

American Seafood

Alaska King Crab
Maine Lobster
Florida Stone Crabs
Chesapeake Bay Crabs
Gulf of Mexico Shrimp
Chincoteague Oysters
Pacific Salmon
Tuna
Dungeness Crabs (Pacific Northwest)

Most of the best American seafood is available around the world by Federal Express. To order Alder Smoked Western Salmon, call Hegg & Hegg of Port Angeles, Washington at (800) 435-3474. Another West Coast delicacy is the Dungeness Crab, available from the Nelson Crab Company, Tokeland, Washington, (800) 843- 8370. On the other coast Florida Stone Crabs are excellent. They are served cold and are available from October 15 to May 15. You can order Florida Stone Crabs by Federal Express from Key Largo Fisheries at (305) 451-3782.

The cold waters off the Maine Coast produce the best lobsters in the world. The Bay State Lobster Company will ship live lobsters anywhere; to order call (800) 225-6240 or (617) 523-7960. The Great Maine

Lobster Company ((800) 222-5033) sells lobsters and the proper tools to cook them. If you want a complete New England Clam Bake (which includes lobster, codfish, mussels, steamers, sausage, potatoes, corn and onions), call Clambakes to Go at (800) 423-4038.

Fresh tuna tastes quite different from canned tuna. However, you can't always get fresh tuna. Ralph Nader, the American consumer advocate, will only eat tuna canned in the United States because he believes our canneries are the cleanest in the world. The best American canned tuna is **Bumblebee** brand solid white tuna. Bumblebee, however, is behind **Chicken-of-the-Sea** and**Starkisk** in making sure that dolphins are not accidentally caught in their nets. Bumblebee claims that it will be "dolphin-safe" within six months.

American Beef, Ribs, Ham and Turkey

American beef is the finest in the world. The best American beef comes from the heartland of the country, an area stretching from Illinois and Nebraska to Texas. Omaha Steaks International will ship high-quality beef to your door ((800) 228-9055, (402) 391-3660).

Virginia ham is an American specialty. The Virginia Provisions Smokehouse will ship you one ((800) 443-7086).

Benjamin Franklin wanted to have the turkey declared the official American bird. The eagle prevailed, but turkey is the official meal of the first truly American holiday, Thanksgiving. Smoked turkey is available from Padows of Richmond, Virginia. Padows also sells excellent Virginia Hams, and can be reached at (800) 344-4257.

Memphis, Tennessee is famous for three things: Elvis Presley, Federal Express and barbecued ribs. Elvis' favorite rib place was Corky's. Corky's will ship its ribs via Federal Express. Place your order at (800) 284-RIBS. The Rendezvous, (901) 523-2746, and John Will's, (901) 274-8000, also ship their ribs via FedEx. The Rendezvous features "dry" ribs, while the other two rib joints barbecue their ribs with sauce. John Will won the Memphis barbecue cook-off two years running.

Kansas City also has claims to the best barbecue. **Arthur Bryant's Barbecue** will not ship out its barbecue sauce or dinners.

Americans are always inventive. The Sun Land Beef Company of Phoenix, Arizona, has recently introduced "Golden Trim" a type of beef which is lower in calories, fat and cholesterol than ordinary beef. In fact it contains less than half the calories of the run-of-the-mill beef, and compares with the calories of skinless chicken. Golden Trim is lower in fat because of breeding and special diet fed to the cows. The product line consists of 27 beef cuts from filet mignon to stewing meat and is the first fresh beef to carry the USDA "Lite" designation. To find out if a retail store near you carries Golden Trim call (602) 279-7977.

☆ ☆ ☆ ☆ ☆

Chapter Twenty-One

All-American Gifts

☆ ☆ ☆ ☆ ☆

This chapter is a collection of gift items which did not fit neatly into any of the other chapters. If you are looking for holiday gift ideas, take a look at this chapter. If you are looking for a gift for a child, turn to the next chapter on toys and games.

Pens

Two of the most famous names in pens are still made in the USA: **Cross** and **Parker**. A pen can be the perfect gift for Mom, Dad, or a recent grad.

A.T. Cross Company has been making writing instruments in the United States since 1846. Today, Cross pens are sold in 150 countries with worldwide sales topping $200 million.

The company sells 83 different styles of pens

ranging from $13 for a chrome mechanical pencil to $800 for a 14K gold fountain pen. Cross sells four basic types of writing instruments: pencil, ballpoint, selectip and fountain pen. Each of these are sold in eight different styles that include in order of price: chrome, gray epoxy, black epoxy, 10K gold filled, 14K gold filled, sterling silver, 14K gold filled and a special series for women.

The Cross for women series is available in each of the first seven styles with additional engraving and a separate soft case for each pen. The company also markets a number of gift sets featuring either one or two writing instruments in an attractive desk top holder. The bases come in a variety of materials such as walnut, onyx, ebony. Depending on the style chosen these gift packages retail for between $95 and $1280; however, the vast majority of the Cross gift sets do sell for under $200, making them an affordable interesting gift idea.

Cross guarantees all its writing instruments mechanically for life. The quality that goes into manufacturing a Cross product is such that fewer than two percent are returned for replacement or repairs.

The Parker Pen Company, founded in 1888 by George Parker, is another famous name in pens. Their first product, the "Lucky Curve" featured an advanced ink feed design. Over a century later, Parker's product line has expanded to 150 different styles, ranging in price from $3.98 to $3,000. Parker is the present world leader in sales of gift and luxury pens. Parker's advertising proudly points out that their pens have been used for everything from writing the Sherlock Holmes stories to the recent treaty signing between Mikhail Gorbachev and Ronald Reagan.

Parker sells many of its writing instruments for

under $100, or even under $50 that make excellent gifts. A number of reasonably priced fountain pens, sales of which have dramatically increased lately, also appear in the Parker catalog. Of course the company does produce an extensive line of gold, silver and lacquer luxury pens retailing for up to $3,500.

Silver, Crystal and China

In 1979 two of the finest names in American silver merged to create **Kirk Stieff**, perhaps the most prestigious name in silver. Samuel Kirk had first made silverware in the Baltimore area beginning in 1815. Charles Stieff did not establish his firm until 1892, but he was just as influential. Samuel Kirk introduced the Repousse style in 1820, featuring that distinctive flower and foliage design that has since become world famous. Kirk silver graced some of the finest American homes including those of Marquis de Lafayette, Robert E. Lee, the Astors and the Roosevelts. On the other hand, Charles Stieff's greatest contribution was influencing the passage of the Silver Laws Registration. This legislation insured that only pieces with at least 92.5 percent fine silver could legally be labeled as sterling silver. Stieff also began crafting authentic reproductions for Colonial Williamsburg in 1939.

Thus the merger joined two of the oldest and most respected American silver firms. Now Kirk Stieff is among the most sought after silver here and abroad. The company manufactures official reproductions for the Smithsonian, Monticello, Old Sturbridge Village, and Historic Charleston as well as Colonial Williamsburg. Kirk Stieff's confidence in its products is backed up by this unconditional warranty: "simply rest assured that if the manufacture of any Kirk Stieff product should be flawed, we are going to replace it."

Kirk Stieff manufactures and sells not only exquisite and expensive pieces of silver and pewter, but also many items that are quite reasonably priced. A stunning example of the best Kirk Stieff has to offer is their sterling silver Repousse waiter. This exceptionally made 22 inch tray retails for approximately $15,000. Rest assured, only a small percentage of the Kirk Stieff catalog falls into that ultra-high price range. An excellent, inexpensive gift from Kirk Stieff might be one of their sterling silver bookmarks which retail for between $10-$20. The bookmarks are available in a boxed and a ribbon style. Another economically priced gift item in the Kirk Stieff catalog is their letter openers ($30) which come in a variety of designs. For those interested in spending slightly more money, Kirk Stieff sells a number of picture frames in silver. The company sells both 3x5 inch ($150) and 8x10 inch ($295) frames.

Lenox crystal and china is world renowned. Lenox makes crystal vases, glassware, dishes, candlesticks and many other beautiful pieces. Lenox makes the highest quality china dishes, tea sets and vases. The company was started in 1887. Lenox designed and produced the official White House china for Woodrow Wilson, and continues to supply the president with china.

Lenox china and crystal stemware is shown above.

A fine crystal piece can always serve as an excellent gift item or estate piece. **Steuben** is the another well-known name in American crystal. A subsidiary of Corning, Steuben was founded in 1903. The company makes all its products in Corning, New York located in Steuben County (hence the name Steuben Crystal). The modern emergence of Steuben took place in 1933 when Arthur Houghton, Jr. (a member of Corning's founding family) took over the Steuben Division. He hired John Gates and Sydney, already well known as an architect and sculptor respectively, to develop a series of designs for the company. These designs were highly received when they were first unveiled in 1935. Even today the company produces nine of their designs, an enduring testament to their quality.

Steuben's newest catalog features hundreds of different pieces in four major categories. The first category is functional forms which includes flower vases, dishes and bowls. Almost all the pieces in this category range in price from $250 to $700. Steuben's line of ornaments includes a variety of offerings; including such pieces as a crystal apple representing New York or love, a crystal and silver rendition of King Arthur's sword Excalibur, or a crystal pendant. A third group in the Steuben line consists of crystal animal figurines. These pieces retail for as little as $135 or as much as $3,150. Finally, Steuben's last line consists of its "major works" exquisite pieces employing their finest craftsmanship. Two examples of this are a piece designed to evoke a cathedral ($13,000) and a work celebrating the New York skyline ($28,500).

Steuben crystal may be ordered on the telephone by calling (800) 223-1234 anytime between 8:30 a.m. and 6:00 p.m. (Eastern time). The company also maintains a store on Fifth Avenue in New York City.

Watches

As with so many products on the market today, what appears to be American is not always so. Watches provide a perfect illustration of this point. Bulova's slogan for its products is "Bulova: America's Time." However, a closer examination revealed that all of their watches are actually imported. There is one company still producing watches in the United States, the **Hamilton Watch Company**. Hand assembled in Lancaster Pennsylvania, Hamilton produces both contemporary and classic styles of watches (all of which have Swiss movements, but American cases, bands and assembly).

Hamilton's largest line of watches is the "traditional classics" line of reproductions of earlier, famous watches from the twenties through the fifties. One of the most striking designs from this collection is the Ventura. Introduced as part of the world's first electric watch line this uniquely shaped design was hailed as a work of art. Hamilton offers an authentic reproduction of the watch produced for the 1928 World Series Champion New York Yankees. This watch has been faithfully reproduced including the engraved caseback which commemorated the Yanks' victory. The Wilshire, Benton and Carlisle are just some of the classic rectangular shaped watches offered in the Hamilton catalog. The Broadway limited is the one pocket watch in the Hamilton line. The watch has an authentic railroad dial that marks each minute separately in red and black numerals. This timepiece can be purchased with one of two different backs: a detailed, embossed image of a steam locomotive or one that allows viewing of the mechanical movements inside. It is a truly classic watch from the best selling railroad watch company of all time.

"Contemporary Classics" feature Hamilton's currently styled watches. The majority of these watches are chronographs, extremely accurate timepieces. As pictured below, Hamilton's chronographs are available with an impressive array of features for an analog watch. The chronographs come with a variety of different dials, bezels and bands. Wordtimer is another member of the Contemporary Classics line; a single glance gives the time in 24 different time zones. By combining function and style this watch is perfect for the business traveler.

Sunglasses

Ray-Ban, the classic American product, is one of the

top names in sunglasses, and has been that way for over 50 years. In the late twenties **Bausch & Lomb** was approached by the Army about developing sunglasses for its pilots. High above the clouds, flyers often encountered brutal glare that caused severe headaches, retching and nausea. Bausch & Lomb developed a green glass that cut glare, checked ultraviolet and infrared rays, and absorbed various colors of the spectrum in a way that allowed the pilots eyes to function naturally. The expectations of the Army were not only filled, but greatly exceeded.

In 1936, Bausch & Lomb decided to begin to commercially market their flying glasses under the name of Ray-Ban. Despite the skepticism of many that no one would pay $3.75 for a product that normally cost $0.25 to $0.50, the glasses were a hit. In their first two decades the glasses were mainly marketed for sportsmen, but beginning around the time the Wayfarer was introduced in 1952, sunglasses were increasingly viewed as a fashion item. The Ray-Ban line gradually expanded to include over 50 different models; the number of choices was reduced to a more workable 16 in 1986.

Sales of Ray-Bans have been increasingly aided by excellent media exposure, and by their identification with certain pop icons. This is most evident with Wayfarer sales which are 50 times greater than in 1981 due to the glasses being associated with the Blues Brothers (John Belushi and Dan Aykroyd) and being featured in the film "Risky Business".

Ray-Ban has been awarded the prestigious Council of American Fashion Designers Award. The current Bausch & Lomb catalog features seven different groups of sunglasses covering a range of styles. These include driving glasses, precious metal frames, leather frames, children's glasses and of course the Wayfarers. The company recently introduced Wings, sunglasses that combine state of the art lenses with modern styling. The protection that is offered in the Wings is so great that Bausch & Lomb patented the design. Ray-Ban lenses all exceed the impact resistance requirement of the Food and Drug Administration (FDA), despite the fact they are all made of glass. The company tests every single lens, not just the batch sample testing required by the FDA.

Cameras

Polaroid has been producing instant cameras for nearly half a century. Today's Polaroid products provide the quality and ease of use always seen in their cameras. Polaroid's flagship product is the **Spectra** system of instant photography. The company believes the Spectra combines the quality of 35mm pictures with the convenience of instant photography. This camera features sonar autofocus and a built-in flash that recharges in as little as 1/5 of a second. The viewfinder also guides the user by signalling "too close," "too far away" or "caution." The Spectra system has a host of accessories that can be purchased. These include five different auxiliary lenses to create multi-images, starbursts or other special effects. Other accessories include a radio controlled remote allowing operation from 40 feet away and a tripod. The camera has a retail price of $225. Accessories range in price from $25 to $40.

Polaroid also markets the **Impulse** cameras which are a more affordable alternative to the Spectra system. The Impulse AF (for Auto Focus) features two different autofocus systems to always capture the best pictures. The Impulse comes with a direct viewfinder meaning that what you see is exactly what appears in the picture. In addition, all the camera functions are controlled by a wafer thin battery contained in the film pack. Polaroid also manufactures a more economical fixed focus Impulse camera that selects the exposure via infrared light. The flash on this camera has an indoor range of from four to ten feet. The Impulse cameras are available in four designer colors. Some Polaroid cameras are imported so watch the labels.

Instantly recognizable, **Kodak** is one of the most famous names in photography. However, Kodak manufactures very few cameras in the United States. Kodak film, on the other hand, is made in the USA and is widely respected around the world.

The largest manufacturer of non-instant cameras in the U.S. is **Keystone** of Clifton, New Jersey. Keystone is the only American which manufactures a complete line of 35mm and 110 cameras and has been making its cameras in the U.S. for over 70 years. The heart of Keystone's product line is their six 35mm cameras. Most of these cameras are focus-free and all have automatic film loading advance and rewind. The top-of-the-line Easy Shot 2AF is equipped with autofocus. Keystone is a solid choice for anyone seeking a modestly priced camera that is made in the USA.

Above is a Keystone Easy Shot camera.

Of the few American-made Kodaks, the most innovative products is the **Fling** disposable 35mm camera.
The basic fling allows for 24 pictures to be taken
before the user returns the whole camera to the
developer. The Fling allows for clear, focused pictures
to be taken from as close as four feet at a shutter
speed of 1/110 of a second. The camera carries a
suggested retail price of about $8 (not including the
cost of developing the film). I tried out a Fling
recently and was amazed at the sparkling clarity of the
pictures.

Other Fling cameras have specialized uses. The
Weekend 35 is aimed at the sports-oriented user with
the power to take pictures at depths up to 12 feet. The
Stretch 35 is a single use camera that takes panoramic
pictures that measure 3 1/2 x 10" when printed.
Previously marketed in both Japan and Europe, the
Stretch 35 just became available in the United States in
the fall of 1989.

Leather Goods

There are many attractive leather products made in America that are excellent gift items. Any person with a hectic schedule would surely appreciate a quality leather date or address book. Other good gift items are luggage, wallets and or purses. Although the preconceived notion is that most leather goods are imported, there exist a number of American companies employing skilled craftsmen who produce excellent goods.

Two excellent manufacturers of date and address books are **Sun Graphix** and **Berman Leathercraft**. Sun Graphix offers a number of fine leather products to aid the busy person in keeping track of their time. These range from a full size desk top planner ($45 in genuine leather) to a compact planner that easily fits into a shirt pocket. The larger planners also include such helpful extras as area code/time zone maps, interest rate charts, population statistics and weather charts.

Coach, based in New York City, is one of the most well-known and respected names in the leather business. Originally only a manufacturer of small leather products, the company has been producing bags and portfolios for a quarter century. Coach developed its own tanning and dying processes which the company believes greatly enhances the leather's characteristics. Coach uses only solid brass fittings manufactured by a century old equine products company. These factors all contribute to the high quality and classic look of Coach products.

A well-made leather briefcase is the type of gift that someone would have to cherish for a lifetime. Philadelphia based, **Schlessinger Brothers** has been making briefcases for almost three quarters of a century.

They claim their standards are so exacting that only five percent of the world's leather is good enough to be used in their products. Additionally, the patented Schlessinger Casesetter frame is made from Spring Steel to insure a strong frame that will last forever. Schlessinger offers a large assortment of styles available in four different types of quality leather. The company offers a limited number of crocodile skin cases which can be special ordered from the company.

Hartman is another American manufacturer of fine briefcases and luggage. *Consumer Reports* rated the Hartman model 4200A4 vinyl case the best of all the briefcases in their survey. The leather Hartman briefcase model 4200EC7 is one of the top cases inspected as well.

Electric Razors

Any father or husband would appreciate a fine electric razor as a gift. **Remington Products** manufacture an excellent product and are an American success story.

Before Victor Kiam, the present owner acquired the company, it had lost an average of $10 million a year for the preceeding three years. Kiam trimmed corporate fat, brought Remington's manufacturing operations home and cut the price of razors by a third. The result? Sales have tripled to three million units a year and the defect rate is near zero. Remington is now the world's number two manufacturer behind Philips' Norelco.

Remington manufactures quality electric razors for both men and women. One of Remington's superior models is the Micro Screen XLR800. This razor produces a quality shave and comes equipped with an excellent trimmer. The BMS-7500 is another highly regarded Remington product; this razor features a special "beard lifter" to gently help cut tough whiskers. For women Remington makes the the Smooth and Silky Women's Electric Razor HR-1. This razor is versatile enough to be able to handle longer hair and stubble.

Cutlery and Lighters

Since 1837 **Lamson & Goodnow** has been manufacturing high-quality knives in western Massachusetts. Lamson & Goodnow now uses high-carbon, non-staining steel for its knives and kitchen tools. In 1990 they introduced a line of topnotch barbecue tools, available in gift boxed sets. To find a Lamson & Goodnow dealer call (413) 625-9816.

If that barbecue fire won't light because of the wind you need a **Zippo** lighter. The Zippo Manufacturing Company of Bradford, PA, has been making the world-famous Zippo lighter for nearly 60 years. George Blaisdell invented this lighter during the depression year of 1932. Since that time the Zippo guarantee still is in force: If a Zippo fails to work the company will fix it for free within 48 hours. Zippos were spread around the world by US soldiers during the second world war. Recently the 200 millionth Zippos was sold. The basic design has not changed, except for a new flint wheel, which will work for as many as 73,000 times.

☆ ☆ ☆ ☆ ☆

Chapter Twenty-Two

Toys and Games

by Debbie Wager

☆ ☆ ☆ ☆ ☆

Toys in this country are not mere amusements, they're big business: Americans spent about $12.75 billion buying these "playthings" in 1988, choosing from about 150,000 different items that are stacked on the nation's toy store shelves.

Most of these toys are not made in this country. In fact, it has been estimated that about 70 percent of all the toys sold here are manufactured elsewhere. Since toys are heavily labor-intensive because of the detail needed for authenticity, painting and assembly, many companies are lured by cheap labor costs to make all their toys offshore. Other firms combine both domestic and overseas production in making an item; still others make different parts of a toy in several locations, and only assemble them here.

Nevertheless, about 45,000 Americans have jobs in the toy industry in the United States, and approximately two-thirds of those are production jobs. Many of the best and most familiar toys are competely made in the United States. What follows, in alphabetical order, are some of the best ones that are Made in the USA.

Breyer Animal Creations make hand-painted, finely-detailed collectible horses. Begun as a custom plastic molding company in 1943, Breyer made its first horse to adorn a timepiece, on commission from a clock company. It then marketed the horse itself, a Palomino, through F.W. Woolworth, and sales zoomed. Since then, Breyer has been producing models of equine legends, all handcrafted at a high level of quality.

The creation process begins on a sculptor's table, where commissioned artists carve the horses out of clay. The sculptors define each detail, from the animals' muscle tone and bone structure to their proportionate size and overall shape. They are then cast in steel and injection molded with cellulose acetate plastic and later hand painted and airbrushed to attain their realistic appearance.

Due to its loyal collector-base of six to 18-year-old girls, Breyer maintains close ties with youth horse activities, including 4-H and Riding for the Handicapped. It also publishes a 32-page magazine, *Just About Horses*, five times a year.

Bubbles. Over 50 million bottles of Mr. Bubbles and Wonder Bubbles are now produced every year in Chicago, Illinois, by the Strombecker Corporation. The wands for the bubble sets, including 10-inch giant wands which can create 8-ft.-long bubbles, are made in their plant in Durant, Oklahoma. Strombecker is now the largest manufacturer of children's bubble products in the world.

Colorforms are flexible, flat, vinyl shapes that children can easily arrange and stick to the sheets of vinyl-covered cardboard that comes with each set; they can be used again and again. The first Colorforms set was created in 1951 by Harry Kislevitz in his apartment in the Bronx, New York; it consisted of basic geometric shapes in primary colors and cardboard dress-up dolls. Today, Colorforms playsets feature scores of licensed characters from Barbie to Mickey Mouse, and are known throughout the world.

Country Critter puppets and stuffed animals are made in Burlington, Kansas. Country Critter is one of the largest puppet makers in the world. Their puppets and stuffed animals are extremely lifelike animals, including pigs, cows, bears, rabbits and more exotic animals. If you have trouble finding these critters in your area call (800) 444-9648.

Crayola Crayons have been made in Easton, Pennsylvania since 1903, when the first box of eight different colored crayons was sold by the Binney & Smith Company for five cents. Schoolteacher Alice Staed Binney coined the term "Crayola" for her husband Edwin's crayons back then, by joining the french word *craie* (stick of color) and *ola* from the word [oleaginous] (oily), because the paraffin wax used in Crayola crayons is an oil derivative.

Today, eighty-eight years later, over two billion

Crayola Crayons are produced by the company each year, in two plants in the United States and in other plants in Canada, England and Mexico.

Binney & Smith still sells a box of eight Crayola crayons (for much more than five cents), but it also sells boxes of 16, 24, 32, 48 and 64 crayons; it has large Crayons for beginners, and So Big Crayons for the youngest artist; regular colors, fluorescent, metallic and pastel colors; wipe-off crayons and anti-roll (flat sided) crayons; colored mechanical pencils in warm shades and cool shades. It also makes markers, paints, brushes, tools, modelling clay, art kits, and coloring books.

Only two crayon color names have changed in the firm's history: in 1962, during the Civil Rights movement, the color called "flesh" was renamed "peach," in recognition of the fact that skin tones span a very wide arc of the color spectrum. And *Prussian Blue* became *Midnight Blue* in 1958, when teachers suggested that students could no longer relate to Prussian history from which the color took its name.

Creative Playthings manufatures more than 20,000 wooden swing sets each year, which accounts for approximately 50 percent of that market, making it the largest manufacturer of wooden backyard playground equipment in the country. The swing sets are well-built and made to last: each one carries a 25-year warranty.

Etch-a-Sketch is made by Ohio Art in Bryan, Ohio, a town 60 miles from Toledo surrounded by fields as flat and precisely tilled as an Etch-a-Sketch drawing.

Invented by Frenchmen Arthur Grandjean, some 50 million units of this self-contained drawing toy have been sold since it was introduced in 1960. Here's how it works: the drawing takes place via a metal stylus that connects the two turning knobs, which control the vertical and horizontal movement. The stylus removes a powdered aluminum and plastic bead mixture from the glass window (now covered with a protective mylar film), causing lines to appear "magically" on the screen; the drawing disappears when the box is shaken.

Wildly popular in the 1960s, and less so in the 1970s and 80s, the company still continues to produce more than 8,000 **Etch-a-Sketch** units a day.

The **Ohio Art Company** was founded by dentist Henry Winzeler in 1908; the first toys were produced during World War I, and included metal tea sets, tops sand pails and drums, all of which are still made.

Fisher-Price is the largest manufacturer of infant and preschool toys in the world. From its beginnings in 1930 in East Aurora, New York, a small village 20 miles from Buffalo, the company has just kept growing.

Known for its brightly colored, durable plastic toys, the first Fisher-Price products were wooden pull-toys named **Granny Doodle** and **Doctor Doodle**. Decorated with brightly colored lithographs, their beaks move and they quack when they are pulled. The whimsical, lighthearted element in those first toys is still a distinguishing trait today.

Although relatively few of its classic toys are completely made and assembled in the United States, their factories in East Aurora and Medina, New York, and in Murray, Kentucky, make several old favorites: the **Rock-A-Stack**, five colorful plastic doughnut-shaped rings that fit over a cone; **Snap Lock Beads**; **Cash Register, Little Snoopy**, and the **Bubble Mower**. The Rock-A-Stack has been around since 1960.

The Bubble Mower is shown above.

Flexible Flyer, the world's most famous sled, became one hundred years old in 1989. The enduring wooden sled, instantly recognizable by its Red Eagle trademark, was invented in 1889 by Samuel Leeds Allen of Philadelphia, a brilliant Quaker businessman who manufactured farm equipment. But production of this equipment was seasonal, and Allen recognized the need for a new product to keep his workers from taking jobs on nearby farms in the off-season.

With a passion for sledding, called "coasting" in those days, and a love of invention, Allen eventually developed and patented a sled which revolutionized the sport. He replaced wooden runners with flexible, T-shaped, steel ones, then fixed the front with a movable, steerable cross-bar, added a slatted seat, and named it the "Flexible Flyer."

The sled was hardly an overnight success: his own salesmen did not like trying to sell it, since the sales season cut their vacations short. And the department store buyers were wary of the new invention, saying they were not practical. But by the early 1900s, with the revival of golf in the U.S. and the increased interest in skating, tobogganing and other outdoor sports, the time was right.

Flexible Flyer sleds are now produced in a new factory located in DuQuoin, Illinois.

All-American Games

Once, there was a real Milton Bradley, who owned a lithography company in Springfield, Massachussets. His best selling product, a picture of a clean-shaven Abraham Lincoln, fell drastically when Lincoln grew a beard, so he created a game to keep his printing company in business. Bradley called it "The Checkered Game of Life," and made the board a checkerboard because he thought life was like that—checkered and uncertain in its outcome. It sold 45,000 copies in 1860, an continued to sell well for several decades.

Today, **Milton Bradley**, in East Longmeadow, Massachusetts, is the largest producer of games and jigsaw puzzles in the world. Most of its board games are completely made in the USA, including **Chutes and Ladders**, where players move up ladders and slide down chutes until one reaches the top, and **Candyland**, which involves color matching.

After a hiatus of many years, Milton-Bradley used "The Checkered Game of Life" as the inspiration for their new Game of Life to celebrate the Company's Centennial in 1960. In a touch of irony, each game reflects its times: "The Checkered Game of Life" was a morality play: if you did the right and virtuous thing, you advanced on the board; the object of the game was to have a happy old age. in [The Game of Life] you choose to go to college, or business; the object is to become a millionaire.

Scrabble is the second all-time top-selling board game in America (after Monopoly). Beginning in 1990, it, too will be a Milton-Bradley game. Invented in 1931 by Alfred Butts to occupy his days of unemplyment during the Great Depression in the 1930s, Scrabble, which started life as Criss Cross, has players pick letters on wood tiles (which are made in Vermont), and form words on a large crossword puzzle board.

It wasn't until 1948 that family friend James Brunot finally convinced Butts that the game had commercial potential, and persuaded him to copyright it as "Scrabble." Today, an estimated two million Scrabble board games are sold annually. The game has been translated into French, German, Hebrew, Italian, Russian and Spanish, and there is even a Braille version.

The dice that are used in most board games are usually manufactured in the Far East. **Pente**, made by Parker Brothers, is played with colored glass stones, and it is completely made in the USA. The object of this family strategy game is to get five stones in a row, or capture five pairs. The game grows in complexity as the skill of the players improve.

Monopoly, the world's best selling game, by Parker

Brothers, was invented during the Great Depression. It uses the streets of Atlantic City, New Jersey, as the properties to be developed. Monopoly has been translated into every major language in the world.

Koosh Ball—named for the sound it makes when it hits your hand—is a natural rubber ball that looks a lot like a porcupine that jiggles. Tactile, soft, bounceless and colorful, the Koosh ball is made with custom, computer controlled machinery in which the rubber goes in one end, and 2,000 fingers of rubber filament Koosh balls come out the other.

The Koosh ball was invented by Scott Stillinger, a computer company engineer, who was frustrated trying to teach his young children how to catch a ball. He and his brother-in-law Mark Button quit their jobs to start **Oddz On Products,** and first introduced the Koosh ball in October, 1987 in California at approximately $5, and it flew off the shelves. By 1989, Koosh was one of the hottest selling toys in the country, with word of mouth (there was little money for consumer advertising) taking it to near the top of the national toy sales charts. With millions sold already, and millions more to come, Koosh has a good shot at being a new American classic.

Above Scott Stillinger (left) and Mark Button are drowning in Koosh balls.

Lauri has been making crepe foam rubber puzzles since 1960. The company began in Haverhill, Massachusetts, then moved to a factory in Phillips-Avon, Maine in 1968. Lauri makes over 150 products for children two to 10 years old, including puzzles, alphabets, numbers, lacing and stringing activities and construction sets. All their products are made in the USA.

The Lauri perception puzzles are particularly good, and are praised for their quality designs. They show groupings of animals, cars and people, each one slightly different from the others in size, type or action. Children must perceive the subtle differences to fit in the pieces.

Lauri's crepe foam rubber pieces are washable and bendable, but they won't curl, crease or tear, and the color doesn't fade. If a piece is lost, the consumer can get a replacement for a $0.50 handling fee.

Lauri's first product, "Fit-a-Space" is shown.

Lincoln Logs, by Playskool, are made in America. Did you know that it takes four train carloads of Ponderosa pine from national forests in Oregon every month to make enough Lincoln Logs to satisfy demand?

They were invented by John Lloyd Wright, son of Frank Lloyd Wright, who got the idea while on a business trip to Tokyo with his father in 1916. As he watched workers move timbers into place for the Imperial Palace Hotel, he was inspired by the Japanese technique for constructing earthquake-proof buildings, and dayreamed of a toy that children could use to build little versions of the structures of America's past—the log cabins, forts and bridges.

Wright worked out details for the toy upon his return to Wisconsin, and in 1918, he put Lincoln Logs on the market. The name was meant to invoke the spirit of Abraham Lincoln, but there wasn't much interest then. By the 1930s, it caught on, and children all over the country were building log cabins. Playskool bought the rights to produce the toy from Mr. Wright in 1943. It now sells about 500,000 sets a year!

Lionel Trains manufactures and markets its famous toy trains out of its headquarters and factories in Mt. Clemens, Michigan. The trains were first developed by the late Mario Caruso, an Italian immigrant who took the primitive battery-powered "box on tracks" invented by Lionel Cowan, and fashioned it into a realistic model train. The train sets were made by the Lionel Corporation from 1900-1969, and then were sold to General Mills Inc., and later were spun off as part of Kenner-Parker Toys.

Train production was moved to Tijuana, Mexico, with disastrous results. As the new plant struggled to maintain quality, it missed delivery dates, irritating retailers. It also vexed model railroad hobbyists like Richard P. Kughn, a Detroit investor who led a group of investors in buying Lionel, and became its chairman. He immediately insisted on moving manufacturing back to its prior base in Mt. Clemens, Mich.

Kughn rehired many of the plant's former workers reemphasizing product quality, and spread the word among enthusiasts that Lionel was back on track. One of their new innovations this year is the Lionel Railscope, a locomotive that has a tiny video camera inside. With it, the engineer can now look down the track just as if he (or she) was sitting in the cab.

Since Kughn took over, Lionel's sales have climbed 150 percent, to $50 million a year. On the average, Lionel makes about one million train engines, cars and cabooses a year.

All **Little Tikes** toys are made in the USA. "We wouldn't have it any other way," said founder and former president Tom Murdough, Jr. The Little Tikes Company was founded in 1970 by Murdough, with nine employees and one rotational molding machine with the iea of producing colorful, durable, plastic playthings in a "Do It Right" atmosphere, and an aim of being not the biggest, but the best.

During the first year, sales were $365,000; in 1988 sales were well over $200 million. Headquarters and manufacturing facilities are located in Hudson, Ohio. The company has been a subsidiary of Rubbermaid since 1984.

Little Tikes is the largest rotational molder of plastic in the world. Its product line has grown from five toys in 1970 to over 150 toys and juvenile products toay. Some of their most popular toys include **Tap-A-Tune Piano; Wee Waffle Blocks. Cozy Coupe Car; Turtle Sandbox** and **Party Kitchen.**

Little Tikes has a strong commitment to customer service. It was the first American toy manufacturer to mold its toll-free number into every product in 1983. In

1988, over 200,000 calls were received by the 25-person consumer service staff. The majority of callers were parents trying to locate a particular product; by giving the operator their zip code, the caller was directed to the closest retailer that carries Little Tikes products.

Magic Slate is an old fashioned cardboard pad, with an acetate sheet you write on and lift to erase. In the early 1920s, R.A. Watkins, the owner of a small printing plant in Illinois, was approached by a man who who wanted to sell him the rights to a homemade device made of waxed cardboard and tissue, on which messages could be printed and easily erased by lifting up the tissue. Watkins had to think about it, and told the man to return the next day.

In the middle of the night, the man called Watkins from jail, and said that if Watkins would bail him out, he could have the rights to his device. Watins agreed and went on to acquire a U.S. patent and rights, as well as the international rights for the device, which he called Magic Slate.

The **Middleton Doll Company** has been making life-like, collectible, limited edition dolls in the Southeastern Ohio since 1978. After careers in police work and private investigation, Lee and Lloyd Middleton decided to begin a new life in evangelism and ministry in the late 1970s.

Middleton Doll is a family operation. Lee and Lloyd work side-by-side producing Lee creations. Her sister Sharon Wells designs some of the doll's clothing. Lloyd also pastors a small Christian church in their community.

Nerf Football, introduced by Parker Brothers in 1972, is 3/4 standard sized football, made of dense foam rubber, and is currently the largest selling football in the world. Capitalizing on soccer's growing popularity in the U.S., Parker introduced the Nerf soccerball, a 3/4-sized version of the standard soccer ball in 1980. The Nerf Turbo Football, new this year, has an aerodynamic design that throws farther, better, and longer than a standard football. All the Nerf products are designed to minimize the injuries and damage that can occur with regulation balls. Other Nerf products that are 100 percent made in the USA include Nerf Fencing, and Nerf Flag Football.

Pinky Balls: remember them from your childhood—those tennis ball-sized, wonderful pink-colored balls that bounced really well? They're made by Hedstrom, in Ashland, Ohio.

Play-Doh is a non-toxic modeling compound that comes in a variety of colors, and stays soft indefinitely, if kept in a tightly-sealed container. Invented by Joseph McVicker, it was introduced by Kenner Toys in 1955, and has become one of the company's oldest and most successful toy lines.

Back then, Play-Doh came in only one color: white; three other colors were added in 1957. And in 1983, the line was expanded to eight colors. Every year, the company introduces several new playsets for the modeling compound, including gadgets like rolling pins and a machine to make spaghetti; extruders that can make shapes like bricks and snakes; and more molds than you can possibly think of. One mold that's been around for years makes it possible for hair to grow out of a character's head.

Kenner Products, a division of Tonka Corporation, still has its factory in Cincinnati, Ohio.

Rocketry is as American as Disneyland. In 1958, soon after the first Sputnik was launched, the Estes Model Rocket Company lifted off in Penrose, Colorado. These working rocket models can go more than 1,000 feet in the air and are reusable. The rockets gently return to earth with the aid of a plastic parachute. Small rockets start at about $3, but you need a launcher and rocket engines. Kits, which include all necessary apparatus, start at about $30. Children enjoy building and painting the rockets as much as the launch itself. These high-tech toys are not recommended for childen under ten. To find a store which carries Estes products call them at (719) 372-6565.

Silly Putty was developed accidentally in a General Electric laboratory during World War II, where scientists were trying to develop an inexpensive synthetic rubber substitute to make Jeep and airplane tires, tank treads and G.I. boots.

Company engineer James Wright worked with boric acid and silicone oil, and created a rubber-like compound with highly unusual properties: the pink substance could stretch like taffy, bounce off walls like a ball, and when struck with a hammer, it shattered like glass. But it was good for nothing the scientists needed, and became a novelty and curiousity on the cocktail party circuit.

Peter Hodgson, a Connecticut marketing man, after seeing silly putty at a party, bought the rights to make it. He packaged half-ounced dabs of the stuff in plastic egg-shaped containers, and sold millions each year. People used it to take lint off clothes, clean typewriter keys, level wobbly furniture, and plug leaks. When he died in 1976 Hodgson left an estate of $140 million.

More than 200 million eggs of Silly Putty have been sold since 1949. In 1977, Binney & Smith, the Crayola people, bought the rights to it; they now produce more than 25,000 eggs, from 600 pounds of silly putty each day; that's about two million "eggs" each year, in their Easton, Pennsylvania plant.

New uses for silly putty are found all the time: receivers for the New England Patriots football team squeeze it to strengthen their hand muscles to help them catch passes; the Apollo 8 astronauts used it during the space flights to fasten their tools during weightlessness.

Slinky: Richard James was a marine engineer aboard ship in 1943 when a torsion spring—a coiled, circular spring—fell off a table and began rolling around the deck. Its wild gyrations amused him and he thought it would make a great toy. James started tinkering with various metals, thicknesses and proportions of metals, and two years later, he perfected a coiled, steel spring (80 feet long if stretched taut), that could spiral from one spot to another and "walk" down stairs. His wife Betty went to the dictionary, and found the name "Slinky."

The Jameses persuaded the Gimbles store in Philadelphia to allow them to set up a sloped board in the toy department, where "Slinky" could walk. Within 90 minutes, all 400 in stock were sold. In 1945, they set up a company, James Industries, in Hollidaysburg, Pennsylvania, and Slinky has kept selling ever since. In the last few years, it has sold at the rate of two million per year. In the late 1970s, they extended the line to include a Slinky Junior, a Plastic Slinky, and Slinky Eyeballs, but the original Slinky still outsells the others.

Teddy Bears, and other stuffed animals, are mostly imported into the United States. We have found two remaining stuffed animal manufacturers, **Country Critter** (mentioned earlier) and the **Vermont Teddy Bear Company**, that makes high-quality stuffed bears and bunny rabbits in its factory in Williston, Vermont. To find a retailer carrying Vermont Teddy Bears call them at (802) 865-4444.

Tinkertoy construction sets were introduced at the 1914 Toy Fair by inventor Charles Pajeau, and caused a tremendous traffic jam when a model was first displayed in a Grand Central Station window. Lockheed once used Tinkertoys as a design model to build an airplane wing fuselage testing system.

Today's Kids makes big, molded plastic toys in a factory in Booneville, Arkansas. The company used to be called Wolverine Toy Company, and it made enamel-finished toy kitchen appliances, and metal and plastic tea sets and dishes. They changed their name in 1986 after switching to colorful, molded plastic for several of their new toys, and they caught on. Their most popular toys include: **All Star Basketball**, a basketball hoop with a patented breakaway rim for slam dunks; **The Merry-Go-Round**, which fits three pre-schoolers comfortably, and has a safety platform and is easy to spin; and **The Busy Center**, which several toddlers can play in and around at the same time. This large toy has nine activities, including two crawl-through areas, a slide, rail track and truck, a shape sorter, xylophone, drop-through chute and a ball raceway.

Tonka, now almost a generic name for sturdy metal toy trucks, took its name from Lake Minnetonka, which dominated the scenery around the company's big factory in Minnesota, its former location. The word "tonka" means "great" in Sioux.

Originally called Mound Metalcraft, it was founded in the basement of a small schoolhouse in 1946. Now Tonka is one of the largest toy companies in the country, owning both Kenner and Parker Toys. Tonka trucks are manufactured in El Paso, Texas.

Video Games. Nolan Bushnell, an American, invented the first video game, **Pong**, is the early 1970s. Now the only video systems made in the USA are games made by **Atari** for video games. Japanese-made Nintendo has taken over the home video market. Atari Games is fighting back. It now makes **Tengen** games in the USA which are compatible with Nintendo. Tengen makes Klax, RBI Baseball, PacMan, PacMania and Ms. PacMan, Afterburner, and many other games. Tengen games are also made for play on home computers, Sega Genesis and NEC TurboGrafx. To find a Tengen retailers near you call (800) 2-TENGEN.

The **Yo-Yo** had its origin as a primitive weapon in the Philippine Islands, long before there was a printed word. It was fashioned from a sharp piece of flint-like rock with a long thong tied to it. If a native's aim was poor, at least the hunter could retrieve the weapon, and the hunting expedition wouldn't be a total loss!

During the 17th and 18th Centuries, the yo-yo evolved into a favorite diversion in the royal courts of Spain and France, and there is even a painting in the Louvre in Paris, of a nobleman holding his yo-yo.

The toy arrived in the United States in the 1920s, where it officially became known as the Yo-Yo. Over half a billion Yo-Yos have been sold in the United States since then.

Duncan Toys makes many of them, in plastic, from its factories in Baraboo, Wisconsin. To find a Duncan Yo-Yo call them at (800) 356-8396.

☆　☆　☆　☆　☆

Chapter Twenty-Three

Tools and Lawnmowers

☆　☆　☆　☆　☆

American-made tools, both hand tools and electric tools, are the best in the world. A few years ago several Japanese power tool makers made inroads into the U.S. market with high-quality, high-priced tools, but the American manufacturers have responded and now produce the highest quality tools at modest prices.

Power Tools

Black and Decker is a good example of how an American manufacturer responded. According to experts in the construction trade who use these tools day-in and day-out, Black and Decker **Industrial** tools, especially drills and saws, are among the best in the world. **Milwaukee** tools generally come in at the top as well. Milwaukee's **Magnum Hole-Shooter** is a tough,

durable drill, made in the USA. Both Black & Decker
and Milwaukee power tools give excellent quality at
reasonable prices, much better buys than Japanese-made
Makita and Ryobi.

Above is Milwaukee's heavy-duty Magnum drill.

Black and Decker has also introduced its
Professional line of drills, saws and sanders, which are
marketed to do-it-yourselfers. For example the Black
and Decker Industrial drill sells for about $120, while
the professional will cost you about $75. B&D also
makes a cheaper line of power tools which sells for
half of the professional line price. **Sears** markets both
the professional and less expensive Black and Decker
power tools under its **Craftsman** label. Unless you give
a power tool heavy-duty use, the less expensive Black
and Decker and Craftsman tools represent an excellent
buy.

Porter-Cable produces the best power sanding

equipment in the world. A Porter-Cable belt sander runs about $400, while its topnotch vibrating sander is only $100.

To hold down wood while working on it with a power tool we recommend the **Hirsh Workstation**. Black and Decker, who invented the similar Workmate, manufactures it in Brazil.

Wagner manufactures a complete line of power tools for painting. It's **PowerRoller** and **PowerPainter** make quick work of painting. The PowerRoller is supplied paint by a tube which makes trips back to the paint pan unnecessary. The PowerPainter is a spray painting system.

Hand Tools

Two American hand tool manufacturers have been making quality tools for over 100 years. The largest hand tool manufacturer is **Stanley Tools**, started by Frederick Stanley in 1843 to produce bolts. Stanley now produces more than 2,000 tools and other products; the company is still based in New Britain, Connecticut.

The other company is **Channellock**, started in 1886 in Conneaut Lake, Pennsylvania by George DeArment, a blacksmith. In 1933 the Channellock tongue and groove adjustable pliers was developed. Channellock now manufactures a complete line of pliers and wrenches of all types.

Sears **Craftsman** hand tools are made in the USA. Sears guarantees these tools indefinitely. If any Craftsman hand tool breaks, for any reason, it will be replaced without question. This guarantee does not apply to Craftsman power tools, and it does not apply to ordinary Sears hand tools, which are often inferior quality tools made in Taiwan. When shopping in Sears for hand tools read the labels carefully.

Some tool manufacturers specialize in producing just one type of tool. For example the **ViceGrip** pliers, a pliers which locks onto its target nut or bolt is the proud product of the Petersen Manufacturing Co. of DeWitt, Nebraska.

Goldblatt manufactures the best drywall tools for finishing, sanding and smoothing joint compound on gypsum materials.

Vaughn and **Estwing** manufacture high-quality hammers. **Wiss** produces topnotch metal snippers.

Shop Accessories

Every good home workshop needs a good tool box. Three U.S. manufactures make high-quality, plastic tool boxes, **Flambeau, Plano** and **Akro Mills.** Flambeau also makes all types of tool organizers and storage bins for tools and hardware. To find a store which carries Flambeau products call (800) 457-5252.

To lock up your toolshed or storage area make sure that you use an American lock. **Master Lock Company,** of Milwaukee, Wisconsin, is the world's largest manufacturer of padlocks, with more than 50 percent of the U.S. market. The **American Lock Company** (Crete, IL) produces a bulletproof lock, similar to the Master Lock, and is the number two U.S. producer. Most other locks are imported, including one called the U.S. Lock.

Brinkmann manufacturers tough flashlights which are useful in your workshop for making repairs in dark places and come in handy when the lights go out. They are made out of anodized aircraft aluminum, are water proof and have an adjustable beam. **Mag Instruments** also produces excellent flashlights.

Brinkmann flashlights are pictured above.

Complete At-Home Workshop

Shopsmith manufactures a complete home workshop in one machine, which is a table saw, lathe, sander and drill press all in one. Shopsmith home workshops start at around $1,500, not for everyone, but for serious woodworking projects. The factory is in Dayton, Ohio, and Shopsmith has about 30 stores around the country. To receive a catalog, or to find a store near you, call (513) 898-9325.

Lawnmowers

Imported lawnmowers are making inroads into the American market. There are many excellent power mowers made in the United States, including **Sears, Jacobson, Cub Cadet, Toro, Lawnboy, Ariens** and

Snapper. *Consumer Reports* gave its highest rating to Sears (model 38023) and Jacobson (model HSD20V). Toro was not tested by Consumer Reports in its latest review of lawnmowers, but has received excellent ratings over the years. Toro also has the most interesting development in lawnmowers, the **Recycler**. The Recycler chops grass very finely so that you do not have to bag clippings. The fine mulch that it creates returns nutrients to the soil so that the need for fertilizers is reduced.

Above is a Toro Recycler.

☆ ☆ ☆ ☆ ☆

Chapter Twenty-Four

Musical Instruments

☆ ☆ ☆ ☆ ☆

American manufacturers produce virtually every type of musical instrument for every budget. Although domestic market share has declined significantly over the past twenty years, the remaining companies command international respect for the instruments that they produce. We have focused primarily on pianos and guitars because they are the most popular instruments in the world.

Pianos

Despite the influx of foreign goods, one area where Americans are making an impact is in the piano market. There are several very good American piano companies producing domestically. In fact, Falcone, which dollar for dollar makes the best pianos in the world, is an American company. Other American companies such as Sohmer, Steinway and Baldwin also manufacture high quality American pianos.

Falcone only began to manufacture pianos this decade, but the company has quickly risen to pre-eminence. Santi Falcone originally owned several piano sales and repair shops; however, he was so disappointed in the quality of today's pianos that he decided to try and manufacture his own. After selling his stores and spending several years doing research and development Falcone began to manufacture his own grand pianos. The company has virtually no advertising, but has received wide spread praise from concert pianists and technicians and is considered one of the world's premiere. Steinway pianos are about 25 percent more expensive than Falcone pianos; Bosendorfer, the top import, is almost twice as expensive as Steinway.

The first name that comes to mind in pianos is likely **Steinway**. The company may only produce 5,000 pianos a year, which is a fraction of the output of some of the large Japanese and Korean manufacturers, but better than 90 percent of the concert artists with major symphonies use Steinways. Three quarters of Steinway's production is devoted to grand pianos which can take up to two years to manufacture and cost between $16,000 and $48,000. The company has risen to the top through exacting quality control and strict attention to detail. Steinway pianos appeal to all types of artists, from classical (Vladimir Horowitz) to jazz (Ramsey Lewis) to pop (Elton John).

A Steinway grand piano is shown above.

Another solid American piano manufacturer is the **Charles Walter Company**. The personal care each Walter piano receives is reflected in the fact that each piano is actually inspected and signed by a member of the Walter family before being sent out. Walter pianos are well designed; each key is individually lead weighted and contains no particleboard in the cabinetry. The Walter is an excellent choice for anybody looking for a well made mid-size American piano that is reasonably priced.

One American manufacturer of pianos that has managed to produce a quality product while still retaining economies of scale is **Baldwin**. The company produces 35,000 pianos annually with a complete range from 36 inch spinets, to nine foot grands. Many Piano experts consider the Baldwin spinet the only one of its type on the market worth considering. Baldwin vertical pianos are better than the average piano for home or school, especially reccomended is the 45 inch Hamilton School or Home Studio ($3,100 for the School and $3,600 for the Home Studio). The availability of the Home Studio in decorator styles is the only difference between the two models. Clearly the best of the Baldwin grand pianos are the seven and nine foot versions which sound as good as any piano on the market.

A final American company that produces a reliable piano is **Sohmer & Co.**; their pianos are marketed under the Sohmer, Mason & Hamlin and Knabe labels. Sohmer's products have a reputation as being well made and of high quality. All Sohmers are made of solid spruce with keys that are individually weighed off. Many piano technicians praise the the quality of the Sohmer. The company also manufactures grand pianos.

Guitars

The lights slowly dim, the band takes the stage and the crowd roars with anticipation. The monstrous speakers erupt with the sound of screaming power cords. Rock and roll and the electric guitar are the Romeo and Juliet of contemporary music. Both are purely American innovations, taken up and developed by foreign firms.

The modern electric guitar for all intensive purposes was invented by Leo Fender in the late 1940s. Prior to this, amplification was accomplished by using a microphone placed in front of an acoustic guitar. This technique created excessive feedback and severely limited the volume and tone of the amplified signal. To this end, Leo Fender revolutionized the sound of music for years to come. Presently, the **Fender** company still exists (without Leo Fender who went on to create Musicman and G&L guitars) having been through several management changes in the past decade. Manufacturing still is based primarily in the USA, with cheaper instruments being imported from the Far East.

The top of the line Fender guitar is a model based on the classic **Stratocaster** form. This guitar, popularized by legends like Jimi Hendrix and Eric Clapton is still popular today, 25 years after the original.

Of equal importance in the history of American contemporary music is the **Gibson Guitar** Company of Nashville, Tennessee. Started over 90 years ago by European immigrants, the company has continuously created top quality acoustic and electric stringed instruments. They have recently reissued the legendary Les Paul Gold Top guitars of the 1950s. These instruments, prized for their sound and craftsmanship, are credited with being the distinctive sound behind the "heavy metal" music popular today.

Above is the famous Fender Stratocaster.

The **Martin Guitar Company** of Pennsylvania has been manufacturing top quality guitars in the United States for over 150 years. Founded by C.F. Martin (an immigrant from Germany) in 1833, the company has grown to a production level of over 20,000 guitars annually. Along the way Martin has earned a reputation for excellence in craftsmanship, design and tonal quality. Their line varies from a $150 student model to some costing several thousand dollars each.

Over the past ten years, several new American man-ufacturers have developed products for the world market. Without exception, they have been in the state-of-the-art side of the industry. **Steinberger Sound** of Putnam county New York developed a plastic resin body guitar, which immediately received praise from the industry. By cutting the weight and redesigning the form of the guitar, musicians are able to concentrate more on the music and less on the instrument itself. Other notable manufacturers include:

Pedulla Instruments, MA
Ken Smith Basses, NY
Alembic Sound, CA
Kurzweil Corporation, MA
Alesis Effects, NY

Keyboards

One of the phenominal success stories of the 1980s has taken place in the small Pennsylvania town of Malvern. From a modest start in 1982, the **Ensoniq Corporation** has grown to over $23 million in sales as of 1989. In the process it has also succeeded in challenging the Japanese corporations at their own game. By pioneering what is called VLSI (very large scale integrated) microchip technology as well as custom software design, Ensoniq applies technology where it had been previously underexploited. And in a short amount of time, Ensoniq has created a strong niche in what had been a Japanese-controlled industry. Its newest product, the VFX, is a state-of-the-art digital keyboard. It combines a programmable synthesizer with reverb and other digital effects along with a 24 track recording system. Ensoniq has created a powerful and user-friendly musical instrument at an extremely competitive price.

The Ensoniq EPS Performance Sampler is shown.

In addition, Ensoniq has applied its knowledge of sound to the hearing aid market. Its new device, the Sound Selector, represents the world's first high-resolution listening instrument. The Sound Selector provides programmability which allows it to match the individual's hearing loss.

David Ash, Vice President of Sam Ash Music, a major American music retailer, recently commented: "If we had more companies like Ensoniq in all fields, with the quality and low price of foreign products, we'd be much more dominant."

INDEX